September 11 Prior Knowledge

Waiting for the Next Shoe to Drop

"NEW YORK, October 12, 2001—I went to Brooklyn this week in search of an 'urban myth' about the World Trade Center attacks. What I came back with was no longer a myth—it was cold, chilling fact. . . . On September 6—five days before the attack—Antoinette DiLorenzo, who teaches English as a second language to a class of Pakistani immigrants [at New Utrecht High School in Brooklyn] . . . witnessed a freshman in her class saying: 'Do you see those two buildings [World Trade Center towers]? They won't be standing there next week.' . . . Moreover, according to police, the youth confirmed having made the September 6 statement about the towers."

—Jonathan Alter, Special to MSNBC

SEPTEMBER 11 PRIOR KNOWLEDGE
© 2002 by Dr. Dennis Laurence Cuddy

Printed in the United States of America

Published by
Hearthstone Publishing, Ltd.
P.O. Box 815 ▪ Oklahoma City, OK 73101
405/948-1500 ▪ 888/891-3300 ▪ *hearthstone@coxinet.net*

ISBN 1-57558-105-1

September 11 Prior Knowledge

Waiting for the Next Shoe to Drop

DR. DENNIS LAURENCE CUDDY

May 21, 2002, memo to FBI director Robert Mueller from FBI senior agent and lawyer Coleen Rowley:

". . . The Minneapolis agents who responded to the call about [Zacarias] Moussaoui's flight training identified him as a terrorist threat from a very early point. . . . While reasonable minds may differ as to whether probable cause existed prior to receipt of the French intelligence information, it was certainly established after that point and became even greater with successive, more detailed information from the French and other intelligence sources. . . . [I have] first-hand knowledge of statements made on September 11, after the first attacks on the World Trade Center had already occurred, made telephonically by the FBI Supervisory Special Agent (SSA) who was the one most involved in the Moussaoui matter and who, up to that point, seemed to have been consistently, almost deliberately thwarting the Minneapolis FBI agents' efforts. Even after the attacks had begun, the SSA in question was still attempting to block the search of Moussaoui's computer, characterizing the World Trade Center attacks as a mere coincidence with Minneapolis' prior suspicions about Moussaoui. . . . HQ personnel brought up almost ridiculous questions in their apparent efforts to undermine the probable cause. In all of their conversations and correspondence, HQ personnel never disclosed to the Minneapolis agents that the Phoenix Division had, only approximately three weeks earlier, warned of al-Qaeda operatives in flight schools seeking flight training for terrorist purposes! . . . I do find it odd that (to my knowledge) no inquiry whatsoever was launched of the relevant FBIHQ personnel's actions a long time ago. Despite FBI leaders' full knowledge of all the items mentioned herein (and probably more that I'm unaware of), the SSA, his unit chief, and other involved HQ personnel were allowed to stay in their positions and, what's worse, occupy critical positions and, what's worse, occupy critical positions in the FBI's SIOC Command Center post September 11. (The SSA in question actually received a promotion some months afterward!). . . . I think you have also not been completely honest about some of the true reasons for the FBI's pre-September 11th failures. Until we come clean and deal with the root causes, the Department of Justice will continue to experience problems fighting terrorism and fighting crime in general. . . ."

Introduction

On page 303 of my book, *The Globalists: The Power Elite Exposed,* published in July 2001 by Hearthstone Publishing, Ltd., I said: "At the national level, this conditioning of the public might be brought about via certain crises, such as a terrorist attack. . . . For the sake of peace and security, people may be willing to give up certain of their freedoms to some extent." Just two months after that book was published, the terrorist attack of September 11 occurred. That very afternoon, ABC News/*Washington Post* released poll results showing that two-thirds of those surveyed "say they would sacrifice some personal liberties in support of antiterrorism efforts."

This book presents some little-known and revealing information surrounding the tragic events of September 11, and it also analyzes how they are among the many steps leading toward the New World Order. For example, it asks why, when hundreds of suspects have been detained here for months, did the FBI help members of the bin Laden family flee the U.S. soon after the attack?

The Times (London)
MON 01 OCT 2001

How FBI helped bin Laden family flee US; War on terror:
Twenty-four members of Osama bin Laden's family were secretly removed from the United States under FBI guard after the terrorist attacks, it emerged yesterday. . . .

Part I

On September 11, 2001, terrorists in airplanes attacked the Pentagon in Washington, D.C., and the World Trade Center in New York City. At about 9:15 p.m. on September 13, CBS news anchor Dan Rather asked Tom Kenney of FEMA what time they arrived in New York, and he replied that they flew in on Monday evening (September 10) and were deployed Tuesday morning. Though he didn't correct himself, nor did Dan Rather, I believe he probably misspoke himself. Nevertheless, it's such statements that fuel conspiracy rumors, such as the reference to the rap group Coup's album cover posted on the Internet July 19 showing the World Trade Center towers with smoke and flames coming out of them. Even earlier, on June 26, a reporter for *indiareacts.com* wrote: "India and Iran will 'facilitate' U.S. and Russian plans for 'limited military action' against the Taliban if the contemplated tough new economic sanctions don't bend Afghanistan's fundamentalist regime. . . ."

Relevant to this "military action," Jim Miklaszewski in his May 16, 2002, NBC News report, "U.S. planned for attack on al-Qaeda," revealed that "President Bush was expected to sign detailed plans for a worldwide war against al-Qaeda two days before September 11." The document was a formal National Security Presidential

Directive, and had to have been in the preparation stage for quite some time prior to September 9 when the president was expected to sign it. One source told Miklaszewski that the directive amounted to a "game plan to remove al-Qaeda from the face of the earth," and it dealt with all aspects of a war against al-Qaeda, ranging from diplomatic initiatives to military operations in Afghanistan. If somehow Osama bin Laden got wind of an impending American attack against al-Qaeda in September 2001, then the September 11 terrorist attacks against the World Trade Center and Pentagon may have been his attempt at a preemptive strike that would, he hoped, rally other radical Muslims in a *jihad* against the U.S. And in case you are wondering how he could have gotten wind of what the U.S. was planning, it is worth noting that in the PBS "Jihad in America" program of 1994, it is shown that the radical Muslims had been able to obtain "classified" U.S. military documents even before 1994.

Miklaszewski reported that the presidential directive

also called for a freeze on al-Qaeda financial accounts worldwide and a drive to disrupt the group's money laundering. The document mapped out covert operations aimed at al-Qaeda cells in about 60 countries. In another striking parallel to the war plan adopted after September 11, the security directive included efforts to persuade Afghanistan's Taliban government to turn al-Qaeda leader Osama bin Laden over to the United States, with provisions to use military force if it refused. . . . [The plan] had been submitted to national security advisor Condoleezza Rice, and the officials said Bush knew about it and had been expected to sign it. The couching of the plans as a formal security directive is significant, Miklaszewski reported, because it indicates that the United States intended a full-scale assault on al-Qaeda even if the September 11 attacks had not occurred.

Some days after the September 11 terrorist attack, noted author Stephen Ambrose questioned how nineteen terrorists could have managed such a detailed and coordinated plan without U.S. government officials becoming aware of it. Good question! This is especially true given that the PBS "Jihad in America" program produced in 1994 showed meetings of radical Muslims in Kansas, Oklahoma, New Jersey, Michigan, and other states, calling for *jihad* (holy war) as far back as 1987. The PBS program also quoted from radical Muslims' documents, giving detailed instructions on attacking our aircraft and saying: "We have to thoroughly demoralize the enemies of God by means of destroying and blowing up the towers that constitute the pillars of their civilization such as the tourist attractions they are so proud of and the high buildings they are so proud of." How could President Bush, Secretary of Defense Donald Rumsfeld, New York City Mayor Rudolph Giuliani and other leaders say no one could have imagined such an attack? We already knew the World Trade Center was a target of terrorists because they tried to bomb it some years ago. And we knew terrorists might use a passenger plane filled with fuel, because that is what terrorist hijackers in Algiers intended to do in 1994 when they planned to fly into the Eiffel Tower exploding the plane over Paris.

The year before the PBS program was produced, prominent globalist and CFR member Arthur Schlesinger, Jr., wrote in the October 27, 1993, *Wall Street Journal:*

Our hasty retreats (e.g., Somalia) tell terrorists everywhere that all they have to do is kill a few Americans and our soldiers will be rushed home. . . . Can the president persuade the nation to let our armed forces do their job in the interests of a new world order? . . . The world of law will not be attained by exhortation. Law requires enforcement. Let us not kid ourselves that we can have a new world order without paying for it in blood as well as in money.

In the same year (1993), Yossef Bodansky (director of the U.S. House of Representatives Task Force on Terrorism and Unconventional Warfare) authored *Target America: Terrorism in the U.S. Today,* in which he described terrorists' training of hijackers and pilots to further *jihad* in the following manner:

The training of suicide pilots started in Busher air base in Iran in the early 1980s. . . . The first installation was established in Wakilabad near Mashhad. . . . According to a former trainee in Wakilabad, one of the exercises included having an Islamic *jihad* detachment seize (or hijack) a transport aircraft. Then, trained air crews from among the terrorists would crash the airliner with its passengers into a selected objective. . . . The leading terrorists are known as "Afghans," having been trained with the *mujahideen* in Pakistan. Some fought in Afghanistan. . . . Muslim volunteers from several Arab and Asian countries were encouraged to come to Pakistan and join the Afghan *jihad.* . . . By the mid-1980s, the Iranian-sponsored Islamist network in the U.S. and Canada had markedly expanded and become better organized. The Islamist infrastructure already included all the components of a mature terrorist support system. These included safe houses in major cities, weapons, ammunition, money, systems to provide medical and legal aid, false identity papers, and intelligence for the operative. The network was also large and spanned the United States.

Bodansky early in 1995 (*before* the Murrah Federal Building in Oklahoma City was destroyed) warned that a federal building in middle America was going to be attacked.

Also in 1993, there was a conference on terrorism at Langley Air Force Base, where terrorists' use of planes was discussed. The conference was organized by Air Force Colonel Doug Menarchik (who now directs the presidential library and museum of former president George Bush) for the Defense Department's Office of Special Operations and Low-Intensity Conflict, and it was titled "Terror 2000." According to Joby Warrick and Joe Stephens in "Before Attack, U.S. Expected Different Hit" (*Washington Post,* October 2, 2001):

Several participants [in the conference] remembered discussing the possibility of a commercial airliner being deliberately flown into a public building in the nation's capitol. . . . "Coming down the Potomac, you could make a left turn at the Washington Monument and take out the White House, or you could make a right turn and take out the Pentagon," Marvin J. Cetron, a Falls Church author and a leader of the exercise, recalled telling the group. A version of the "Terror 2000" report marked "interim draft" correctly predicts several aspects of the September 11 attack. "In the future, horrified civilians will get to watch

—10—

every step in a terrorist plot," it says. "CNN and other networks will certainly air the footage." Presaging a break from the state-sponsored terrorism familiar to most Americans at the time, the report said tomorrow's "most dangerous" terrorists would be "motivated not by political ideology but by fierce ethnic and religious hatreds. Their goal will not be political control but utter destruction of their chosen enemies," it said.

And in *The Futurist* (November/December 1994), Marvin J. Cetron and Owen Davies wrote in "The Future Face of Terrorism" that

targets such as the World Trade Center not only provide the requisite casualties but, because of their symbolic nature, provide more bang for the buck. In order to maximize their odds for success, terrorist groups will likely consider mounting multiple, simultaneous operations with the aim of overtaxing a government's ability to respond, as well as demonstrating their professionalism and reach.

Closer to September 11, 2001, according to an Associated Press column, "Key Suspect Had Been Under German Surveillance" (September 29, 2001) by David Rising, hijacker Mohammed Atta had been under CIA surveillance in Frankfurt, Germany, from January to May 2000, after which he came to the U.S. in June 2000 for flying lessons. The question is why was Atta important enough for the CIA to watch him in Germany, but supposedly no American officials thought it important enough to monitor him once he came to the U.S.?

Another question is raised by an October 4, 2001, indictment of Osama bin Laden by the British government. The indictment is titled "Responsibility for the Terrorist Atrocities in the United States, 11 September 2001," and in it one finds: "In August and early September close associates of bin Laden were warned to return to Afghanistan from other parts of the world by 10 September. Immediately prior to 11 September some known associates of bin Laden were naming the date for action as on or around 11 September." If intelligence authorities were aware of the specificity of these dates, why was nothing done to prevent the attacks? Apparently there was never even any contingency planning about what preventive measures to take (e.g., a military helicopter placed on standby alert) if the World Trade Center was attacked again by whatever means, including a suicide airplane attack.

Also regarding specific dates, according to "Bin Laden Told Mother to Expect 'Big News'" (London *Daily Telegraph,* October 2, 2001), by Ben Fenton and John Steele, Osama bin Laden called his stepmother on September 9 and said, "In two days you're going to hear big news and you're not going to hear from me for a while." And according to NBC News, this phone call was intercepted by a "foreign intelligence service." Shouldn't one assume that this foreign intelligence service would have shared this information with American intelligence officials?

The day after bin Laden made this phone call, the Congressional Research Service on September 10, 2001, issued a report titled "Terrorism: Near Eastern Groups and State Sponsors," in which one reads the following:

Signs continue to point to . . . a rise in the scope of threat posed
by the independent network of exiled Saudi dissident Osama

bin Laden. . . . Osama bin Laden's network, which is independently financed and enjoys safe haven in Afghanistan, poses an increasingly significant threat to U.S. interests in the Near East and perhaps elsewhere.

The report also indicated "that the network wants to strike within the United States itself."

Also on September 10, U.S. intelligence agents intercepted a call between "bin Laden supporters in the United States and senior members of bin Laden's al-Qaeda terrorist organization" in which they discussed an upcoming "big attack." This is according to an article, "Intercepts Foretold of 'Big Attack'" (*Washington Times,* September 22, 2001), by Rowan Scarborough, who identified the source of this information as "a senior administration official."

Within hours of the terrorists attack on September 11, 2001, ABC News/*Washington Post* released poll results showing two-thirds of those surveyed "say they would sacrifice some personal liberties in support of antiterrorism efforts." In my booklet, *Conspiracy,* published some years ago by Florida Pro Family Forum, Inc., I wrote about the future, saying that " . . . actual terrorist attacks upon buildings, airplanes . . . were used by The Order to justify greater monitoring of the population's activities along with the confiscation of all firearms. In public areas, video and audio monitors were placed on all streets and buildings. . . ."

Years before the September 11 attack, Richard Haass (director of national security programs at the Council on Foreign Relations) wrote in a *Washington Post* op-ed column that in the war against terrorism, there will have to be "a willingness to compromise some of our civil liberties, including accepting more frequent phone taps and surveillance. Those who would resist paying such a price should keep in mind that terrorism could well get worse in coming years." And just six days after the September 11 attack, the *Orange County Register* (September 17) published an Associated Press article, "More Security, Less Liberty" by Anick Jesdanun, in which one reads:

> Even before Tuesday's attacks, some in government sought greater surveillance powers over e-mail and telephone communications. . . . "The intelligence agencies have a long list of things they want done," said Morton Halperin of the Council on Foreign Relations in Washington, D.C. "They've been waiting for an event to justify them."

In 1928, the "Father of Public Opinion," Edward Bernays, authored *Propaganda* in which he said that politicians and businessmen should take "a survey of public desires and demands," in order to say "I must lead the people. Am I not their servant?" Bernays went on to say that

> those who manipulate the organized habits and opinions of the masses constitute an invisible government which is the true ruling power of the country. . . . It is they who pull the wires which control the public mind, who harness old social forces and contrive new ways to bind and guide the world. . . . As civilization has become more complex, and as the need for invisible government has been increasingly demonstrated, the technical means have been invented and developed by which opinion may be regimented.

In 1928, Bernays also became the chief adviser to CFR member William Paley, who was beginning CBS.

The diminution of national sovereignty has long been a goal of the power elite, and after the September 11 terrorist attack, the *New York Times* (September 24, 2001) published Robert Wright's "America's Sovereignty in a New World," in which he wrote that "the war on terrorism truly is of a wholly new kind—that it must be fought on many fronts, including the creation of international policing mechanisms that could impinge on national sovereignty as never before." And five days later, Canadian prime minister Jean Chretien said regarding the terrorist attack: "There will probably be a new order in the world that will probably be better than we have now" (*Toronto Star,* September 30, 2001).

Regarding the psychology of how the power elite can get the people to accept a diminution of our national sovereignty, psychiatrist William Sargant wrote in *Battle for the Mind: The Mechanics of Indoctrination, Brainwashing, and Thought Control* (1957) that "belief can be implanted in people after brain function has been sufficiently disturbed by . . . induced fear, anger, or excitement. Of the results caused by such disturbances, the most common one is temporarily impaired judgment and heightened suggestibility." That people should perhaps be willing to give up some of their liberties because of their desire to avoid future terrorist attacks is a form of "psychological retreat." According to former Tavistock senior staff member Fred Emery's "theory of social turbulence," people will go into psychological retreat after being faced with a series of emotional or other crises. After the September 11 terrorist attack, Attorney-General John Ashcroft requested sweeping surveillance powers, but U.S. Rep. John Conyers said that he and others were "deeply troubled" by the constitutional implications of this, and he noted that "past experience has taught us that today's weapon against terrorism may be tomorrow's law against law-abiding Americans."

Does all of this mean that the power elite plotted the terrorist attacks of September 11? No, they didn't have to. You may recall that Cecil Rhodes' conspiracy to take the government of the whole world was planned to end after about six decades. That is because by that time, they believed they would have enough like-minded globalists in place in areas such as politics, economics, education, and journalism, that a conspiracy would no longer be necessary. The power elite supports greater gun control, so to show how this works, in the field of journalism, for example, when a student several years ago went on a shooting rampage, the press rarely reported that he was stopped by a teacher who had a gun, because the press is overwhelmingly for gun control. The power elite did not have to call editors of the nation's newspapers and tell them what to say.

Similarly, the power elite didn't call up terrorists and tell them to fly into the Pentagon and World Trade Center. However, if I could forecast terrorist attacks, so can the power elite.

Rather, there is a dialectic at work here. You may recall that under a State Department contract, CFR member Lincoln Bloomfield in 1962 wrote:

> A world effectively controlled by the United Nations is one in which "world government" would come about through the establishment of supranational institutions, characterized by . . . some ability to employ physical force. . . . [But] if the commu-

nist dynamic was greatly abated, the West might lose whatever incentive it has for world government.

Relevant to today, it is the *reaction* (public willingness to give up some constitutional freedoms) to the *action* (terrorist attack wherever and whenever and however it occurs) that is important to the power elite. Thus, they don't have to cause the action, but only anticipate that it will occur sometime, and emphasize the public reaction to it to further their goals. And in case anyone doesn't believe the power elite wants a diminution of our constitutional freedoms and our national sovereignty, just look at *Our Global Neighborhood: The Basic Vision,* a document produced several years ago by the Commission on Global Governance, whose work was supported by then U.N. Secretary-General Boutros Boutros-Ghali. Members of the commission included Maurice Strong (secretary-general of the Rio Earth Summit, co-author of the current Earth Charter, and right-hand man of U.N. Secretary-General Kofi Annan) and Barber Conable (former president of the World Bank). And among the commission's proposals are that

> a new world order must be organized. . . . In certain fields, sovereignty has to be exercised collectively. . . . The principle of sovereignty must be adapted in such a way as to balance . . . the interests of nations with the interests of the global neighborhood. . . . We strongly endorse community initiatives to . . . encourage the disarming of civilians. . . . We would like to see a permanent international criminal court instituted as a matter of the highest priority. . . . We are . . . in need of a mobilizing principle . . . a new world order that secures the ascendancy of global neighborhood values over divisive nationalism.

It is important to remember that the power elite is neither exclusively liberal nor exclusively conservative. Their goal is power and control. As former communist Dr. Bella Dodd wrote in *School of Darkness* (1954), "Today I marvel that the world communist movement was able to beat the drums against Germany and never once betray what the inner group knew well: that some of the same forces which gave Hitler his start had also started Lenin and his staff of revolutionists." She also wrote that "the progressive businessmen were playing a revolutionary role." The power elite and their globalist goals must be resisted by Americans who oppose any diminution of our constitutional freedoms or our national sovereignty.

While there is a lot of flag-waving today, one wonders whether this reflects a genuinely deep patriotism. After all, if on September 10 someone had stood on a street corner waving the American flag and saying he or she is a patriot, the person probably would have been considered by many to be a right-wing reactionary. Will most of the people now waving the American flag after September 11 buy American-made cars instead of those made overseas? And will they now buy American-made clothes and toys instead of those made in Communist China? I doubt it.

It is true that the terrorists of September 11 did engage in "an act of war" and that they should be "brought to justice." But did we call it "an act of war" when the Clinton administration sent a cruise missile into a medicine factory in the Sudan, killing a lot of innocent, poor, African Muslims? And did we say the Clinton administration officials responsible for that should be "brought to justice"? No. Those officials simply said they believed they were attacking a facility that made material used for weapons, though they couldn't conclusively prove it and independent scientific investigative bodies couldn't prove it either. Do we really want a world in which country "X" believes country "Y" is producing something dangerous and is therefore entitled without proof to bomb a medical facility there? I don't think so, and I don't think we would accept that if some country did it to us. And suppose some country arrested former President Bush because he violated their nation's laws, just as he invaded Panama and arrested Manuel Noriega for violating American law—would we accept that? Again, I believe the terrorists of September 11 are murderers who should be brought to justice, but until we cease using double standards, the terrorists of the world will use our hypocrisy to gain recruits against us. Please pray that America will return to the biblical values upon which this nation was founded.

After September 11, 2001, many Americans unfortunately seem willing to give up some of our freedoms (e.g., privacy rights) for security, and on May 30, 2002, U.S. Attorney-General John Ashcroft announced that restrictions on the FBI's domestic spying and surveillance of religious and political organizations would be relaxed. Undercover agents would be able to investigate churches, for example, *without* having probable cause or evidence leading them to believe someone in the church may have broken the law.

Part II

In Part I of this book, I offered some analysis of why the September 11, 2001, terrorist attacks upon the World Trade Center (WTC) and the Pentagon occurred, and this part will continue that analysis. However, it is important first of all to know the background leading up to the events of early September.

Cecil Rhodes' conspiracy to take control of the world was to last about six decades as something hidden or secret, after which it was to become what H. G. Wells referred to as an "open conspiracy" with Rhodes scholars such as Walt Rostow, Senator J. William Fulbright, Richard Gardner, Strobe Talbott, and Bill Clinton *openly* calling for a reduction in national sovereignty and/or supporting a world government.

Wells was an important advocate of world government, and in 1933 published *The Shape of Things to Come,* in which he foretold that World War II would begin in about six years. How did he know there would be a second world war? In the same year he published his *The Open Conspiracy: Blue Prints for a World Revolution* (1928), Wells received a letter from Fabian Socialist Bertrand Russell (who in the early 1950s wrote of the need perhaps for bacteriological warfare to further their population control objectives). In the letter, Russell indicated that Lord Haldane (who was involved in

Rhodes' plan) "would not forego the pleasure to be derived from the next war." This does not mean the conspirators called up Hitler and told him to invade Poland in 1939, but rather as I indicated in the preceding part of this book, they create conditions from which it is rather easy to foretell that an action will occur, and the power elite will use the reaction to that action to further their objectives. In the case of World War II, the power elite helped to finance Hitler's ability to create a war machine.

In *The Shape of Things to Come,* Wells also wrote that after the Second World War, there would be an increasing lack of safety in "criminally infected" areas. Again, how does Wells know this? Why doesn't he predict that after the war, people will be so tired of stress and violence that they will just all agree to have peace and love one another? No, Wells knew that he and his power elite allies would promote humanistic values throughout societies. This "do your own thing" value system would naturally result in an increase in crime, and this action would result in a public reaction that would accept more government controls, and eventually a world government to combat international crime/terrorism.

Concerning the terrorist attacks of September 11, did the power elite know something might happen? In Part I of this book, I quoted from a 1962 document, "A World Effectively Controlled by the United Nations," by CFR member Lincoln Bloomfield. The document was prepared under a State Department contract (Number SCC 28270), and Rhodes scholar Dean Rusk was secretary of state. Relevant to September 11, 2001, it indicated that world government could come about by means of "a grave crisis or war to bring about a sudden transformation in national attitudes sufficient for the purpose. . . . The order we examine may be brought into existence as a result of a series of sudden, nasty, and traumatic shocks." Could one possible example of this be airplanes flying into buildings killing thousands, followed by anthrax in the mail?

But why did the terrorist attacks of September 11 occur now? There have been many terrorist attacks in the past, including the Black Hand's assassination of Austrian archduke Franz Ferdinand that precipitated World War I. However, the attacks upon the U.S. today are different primarily because of the far-reaching al-Qaeda terrorist network funded by Osama bin Laden. And what upset him so greatly? Was it Israel? No, Israel is secondary to him. What got him most upset was that during the Gulf War in 1991, American military forces came to his country of Saudi Arabia, and remained there. He saw it as "infidels" desecrating Muslim holy land, and he saw it as the United States protecting the dictatorial elite of Saudi Arabia (if one even protests there, he or she is sent to prison). And who is behind the protection of the Saudi elite? It is the globalist power elite. They did not direct nineteen terrorists to attack the World Trade Center and the Pentagon on September 11. Rather, they create conditions from which one can foretell that a reaction might occur.

And in case anyone questions whether the Bush administration supports the Saudi elite today, one might read in the October 1, 2001, *London Times* "How FBI helped bin Laden family flee U.S." At a time when literally hundreds of people who might have knowledge related to the terrorist attacks of September 11 are being detained by American authorities, this article shows dramatically different treatment for the Saudi elite, including the bin Laden family. The article says:

> Twenty-four members of Osama bin Laden's family were se-
> cretly removed from the United States under FBI guard after
> the terrorist attacks. . . . Immediately after the attacks they were
> taken under FBI escort to Texas. From there they went to Wash-
> ington, D.C., and the safety of the Saudi Embassy. As soon as
> U.S. airports reopened, the relatives were flown back to Saudi
> Arabia.

The article also states that the departure was organized by Prince
Bandar bin Sultan, Saudi Arabia's ambassador to Washington, who
is "a leading Washington figure with close ties to the Bush family."
About one hundred forty members of the Saudi royal family were
also sent home. How could U.S. officials know so quickly that
none of these people had any knowledge pertaining to the terrorist
attacks?

Concerning the globalist power elite's support for the Saudi
elite, in Holly Sklar's book *Trilateralism: The Trilateral Commission
and Elite Planning for World Management* (1980), there is an essay
titled "Co-opting the Third World Elites: Trilateralism and Saudi
Arabia" by Kai Bird, who has written for liberal publications such
as the *Washington Post* and the *Los Angeles Times,* and who was assistant editor of the leftist publication *The Nation* at the time this essay was written. In the essay, Bird quoted Tim Farer in the CFR's
Foreign Affairs (October 1975) as explaining how co-opting certain
people has worked in the past: "There was a creaming off and co-
optation of the natural elite of the working class [in America]. Some
members were drawn off early by opening the channels to higher
education." And regarding "Third World elites," Farer related the
benefits of having only a small number who have to be co-opted.

Bird then stated:

It is in this context that our relationship to the Arab oil produc-
ers—and Saudi Arabia in particular—is considered of crucial
importance by the trilateral policy makers. . . . The goal of U.S.
diplomatic efforts in the Middle East is not to lower oil prices
but to insure stable supplies. . . . Saudi Arabia controls the en-
tire system [OPEC]. . . . Dr. Mason Willrich, director of the
International Division of the Rockefeller Foundation, told an
audience of energy experts at Princeton University: "In discus-
sions we have had with our European and Japanese allies, they
have emphasized that they want the United States committed
to stable Saudi imports—for their own protection." The major
strategy, according to the trilateralists, is to entangle the Saudis
with the Americans and assure them a stake in the established
economic order.

Bird then explained that the Saudi elite used their profits to pur-
chase U.S. Treasury bonds and corporate securities as well as U.S.
goods and services. One of the pillars of the special relationship
between the American power elite and the Saudi elite is the Arabian American Oil Company (ARAMCO), representing Mobil,
Exxon, Texaco, and Standard Oil of California. Bird indicated that
ARAMCO "has created a company state in Saudi Arabia" working
with "the Saudi elite," and "thus unknown to the American people
—and without any real public debate—quiet alliances are being
negotiated [supposedly on their behalf] to secure necessary natural resources, and oil in particular, that are controlled by the autocratic elites of a few regional Third World powers."

Whenever we have supported autocratic elites in the past, there have eventually been revolts against the Third World autocrats and resentment against America for having propped them up. Thus, it was not difficult for the globalist power elite to foretell there would eventually be a reaction to our military support for the Saudi elites. And within hours of the September 11 terrorist attacks on the World Trade Center and the Pentagon, ABC News/*Washington Post* released poll results showing that at least two-thirds of the Americans surveyed would be willing to "sacrifice some personal liberties in support of anti-terrorism efforts." This was foretold in "Prepare now for terrorist attacks, or get ready for martial law," published in the *Charlotte Observer,* February 6, 1999 (reprinted from *Newsday,* February 3, 1999). The article was by Neil Livingstone, chief executive of GlobalOptions, a crisis management company, and in it he stated regarding a possible future terrorist attack upon the U.S.:

> The greatest risk will be to our civil liberties. If the nation is not adequately prepared for such an attack, the public is likely to panic and demand that lawmakers take whatever measures are deemed necessary at the time to respond to the crisis, irrespective of the Bill of Rights and the Posse Comitatus Act. Governors will call out the National Guard, . . . and federal troops will be deployed in the streets of our towns and cities.

Relevant to this is William Safire's "Seizing Dictatorial Power" in the *New York Times* (November 15, 2001), concerning President Bush's proposed establishment of a military tribunal to deal with aliens accused of involvement in terrorism. The nationally syndicated Safire wrote:

Misadvised by a frustrated and panic-stricken attorney general, a president of the United States has just assumed what amounts to dictatorial power to jail or execute aliens. Intimidated by terrorists and inflamed by passion for rough justice, we are letting George W. Bush get away with the replacement of the American rule of law with military kangaroo courts. . . . Not content with his previous decision to permit police to eavesdrop on a suspect's conversations with an attorney, Bush now strips the alien accused of even the limited rights afforded by a court-martial. His kangaroo court can conceal evidence by citing national security, make up its own rules, find a defendant guilty even if a third of the officers disagree, and execute the alien with no review by any civilian court. . . . It's time for conservative iconoclasts and card-carrying hard-liners to stand up for American values.

That ABC News/*Washington Post* would survey the public's willingness to sacrifice some personal liberties so quickly after the September 11, 2001, attacks has led to conspiratorial questions about the power elite's control of the media. Therefore, it was not surprising when *ABCNews.com* on April 17, 2002, published online a story attempting to debunk conspiracy theories. The story, "What Consensus? Conspiracy Theorist Immune to the Widespread Support for War on Terror" by Dean Schabner, refers to "conspiracy mongers," and indicates that "in conspiracy theories, . . . often there is some leap, a break in the chain of logic from a series of facts to the conclusion."

Americans' willingness to give up some of our liberties in support of anti-terrorism efforts is absolutely essential to the power elite's goal of world government. But we would do well to remember these words of Benjamin Franklin quoted from the *Historical Review of Pennsylvania* in 1759: "They that can give up essential liberty to obtain a little temporary safety, deserve neither liberty nor safety."

Was it foreseeable that a terrorist attack would occur in the U.S. on September 11? In the first place, the State Department manual concerning visas has stated that "mere membership" in a recognized terrorist group, or even "advocacy of terrorism," doesn't automatically disqualify a person from entering the U.S. Therefore, it was no surprise that terrorists were here. Secondly, after the bombing of the World Trade Center in 1993, Philippine authorities in Manila arrested Abdul Hakim Murad, a follower of Osama bin Laden, and found a plot, "Project Bojinka," on his laptop computer to hijack U.S. airliners. In an article, "Similar Plot Uncovered in Philippines, says Police Chief" (*Sydney Morning–Herald,* September 13, 2001), one learns that Manila police chief Avelino Razon told Agence France-Presse: "I remember that after the first World Trade Center bombing, Osama bin Laden made a statement that on the second attempt they would be successful."

American officials were made aware of the Project Bojinka plot which, according to *Washington Times* reporter Bill Gertz, involved crashing the planes specifically into the WTC, Pentagon, the White House, and other targets. This was discovered in 1995, and three years later the leading paragraph of a Reuters news release on August 21, 1998, stated: "A furious Muslim world on Friday issued warnings of a bloody backlash against the United States over its missile strikes on targets in Afghanistan and Sudan." The next year, in September 1999, a report titled "Sociology and Psychology of Terrorism: Who Becomes a Terrorist and Why?" was completed by the Federal Research Division (an arm of the Library of Congress) for the National Intelligence Council. The report, authored by Rex Hudson, warned that Osama bin Laden's al-Qaeda network might seek revenge for the American air strikes against bin Laden's camps in Afghanistan. Hudson further speculated:

> Suicide bomber(s) belonging to al-Qaeda's Martyrdom Battalion could crash-land an aircraft packed with high explosives (C-4 and semtex) into the Pentagon, the headquarters of the Central Intelligence Agency (CIA), or the White House. . . . Ramsi Yousef had planned to do this against the CIA headquarters.

The same year, on December 6, 1999, former U.S. Senator Gary Hart, co-chairman of the U.S. National Security Commission for the 21st Century, said at the Yale Center for International and Area Studies that the U.S. would be attacked on its own soil mostly by a small group of foreign terrorists, and that attack could result in the loss of many American lives. Co-chairing the commission with Hart (who recently received his Ph.D. from Oxford University) was former U.S. Senator Warren Rudman (CFR member). Both Hart and Rudman attended a meeting of the Council on Foreign Relations in Washington, D.C., three days after the September 11, 2001, terrorist attack. And at the meeting, Hart said: "There is a chance for the President of the United States to use this disaster to carry out . . . a phrase his father used, . . . and that is a new world order."

On June 23, 2001, on *AirlineBiz.com,* flight attendants could read that two days after interviewing Osama bin Laden, Arabic satellite television channel MBC reported: "There is a major state of mobilization among the Osama bin Laden forces. It seems that there is a race of who will strike first. Will it be the United States or Osama bin Laden?" What was meant by this reference to "who will strike first" was mentioned in Part I of this book, and refers to a June 26, 2001, *indiareacts.com* article referring to an upcoming joint military operation by the U.S. and Russia against the Taliban "if the contemplated tough new economic sanctions don't bend Afghanistan's fundamentalist regime." The article goes on to say that this is connected to who will control the "vast oil, gas, and other resources" of Central Asian countries. In case one believes that this is a farfetched idea, note that at the end of his ABC "Nightline" program on April 26, 2002, host Ted Koppel stated: "It is important to remember that Washington has its eye on more than just the global war on terrorism. Oil and gas in vast quantities are available in Central Asia. The U.S. national interest is deeply invested in gaining permanent access to those supplies."

Further connecting oil to the current war between the U.S. and its allies against the Taliban is Reuters reporter Tahir Ikram's article "Taliban offer two million to die for Afghanistan" (October 9, 2001) in which he wrote:

> U.S. oil companies have been interested in tapping the vast oil and gas resources of Central Asia since the Soviet Union collapsed in 1991 but have run into troubles piping it out. Washington opposes a pipeline through Iran, leaving the route through Afghanistan the best alternative. It supported the Taliban when they seized power in 1996 because they seemed capable

of assuring the peace that investors would need. But Washington soon soured on the Taliban because they harboured bin Laden.

Supporting the contention made in the June 26 *indiadirects.com* article is the following item, titled "US 'planned attack on Taleban,'" by George Arney of the British Broadcasting Corporation (BBC) on September 18, in which one reads:

A former Pakistani diplomat has told the BBC that the U.S. was planning military action against Osama bin Laden and the Taleban even before last week's attacks. Niaz Naik, a former Pakistani Foreign Secretary, was told by senior American officials in mid-July that military action against Afghanistan would go ahead by the middle of October. Mr. Naik said U.S. officials told him of the plan at a U.N.-sponsored international contact group on Afghanistan which took place in Berlin. Mr. Naik told the BBC that at the meeting the U.S. representatives told him that unless bin Laden was handed over swiftly America would take military action to kill or capture both bin Laden and the Taleban leader, Mullah Omar. The wider objective, according to Mr. Naik, would be to topple the Taleban regime and install a transitional government of moderate Afghans in its place. . . . Mr. Naik was told that Washington would launch its operation from bases in Tajikistan, where American advisers were already in place. He was told that Uzbekistan would also participate in the operation. . . . Mr. Naik was told that if the military action went ahead it would take place . . . by the middle of October at the latest. . . . He said it was doubtful that Washington would drop its plan even if bin Laden were to be surrendered immediately by the Taleban.

Might knowledge of the immediately aforementioned have prompted the attacks of September 11, with bin Laden and the Taliban hoping that an American military response would result in a *jihad* against the U.S. by Muslims around the world?

Closer to September 11, the *London Times* (September 27) reported that on September 3, "the Federal Aviation Authority made an emergency ruling to prevent Mr. [Salman] Rushdie from flying unless airlines complied with strict and costly security measures. . . . The FAA told the author's publisher that U.S. intelligence had given warning of 'something out there' but failed to give any further details." And according to the *San Francisco Chronicle* (September 12), San Francisco mayor Willie Brown was to fly from that city to New York City the morning of September 11, but he "got a call from what he described as his airport security—a full eight hours before yesterday's string of terrorist attacks—advising him that Americans should be cautious about their air travel." Given all these warnings, apparently no one was even placed on the top of the WTC with small rockets or armor-piercing bullets to try to prevent an air attack upon the buildings.

Again, it is important to remember that the power elite did not direct nineteen terrorists to fly planes into the WTC and Pentagon. Rather, they simply are able to foretell that some action (e.g., a terrorist attack) might occur because of their support of the Saudi dictatorial elite, and they use the reaction of the American people (greater willingness to give up some liberties in exchange for peace and safety) to further their goals.

Four days after the terrorist attacks, Marcus Mabry's September 15 *"Newsweek* Web Exclusive" was titled "Welcome to the New World Order." And in David Broder's *Washington Post* (October 14) column, "Wonders of a New World," he quoted U.S. Senator Pete Domenici as saying, "We may have a 'new world order' without anyone having asked for it."

And what is the New World Order that the power elite wants? It is a world government brought about via regional economic arrangements globalized into a global economy that the power elite will say has to be managed by a world government.

Regarding regional economic arrangements, they have been under way for some time now. In David Crane's *Toronto Star* (November 21, 1992) article, "New nation called Cascadia rising on both sides of border," he wrote that

> a new almost-a-country is developing out on the West Coast and it includes a big chunk of Canada. This is Cascadia, a region that includes the states of Oregon, Washington, Idaho, western Montana, and Alaska, along with the provinces of British Columbia and Alberta, as well as parts of the Yukon and Northwest Territories. . . . It is . . . the product of a changing world and global economy. It's also a reflection of the way in which regions are taking more control over their futures regardless of whether national boundaries exist. Cascadia, for example, sees much of its future potential coming from its links with Asia and even Europe, and not with other parts of Canada or the United States. . . . Institutional arrangements are emerging that could lead to Cascadia operating in the rest of the world as almost a country. . . . The next step, [regional planner Paul]

Schell suggests, is the formation of some kind of regional council to formalize the relationship between the participating states and provinces. . . . The Pacific Northwest Economic Region is one forum that already exists, for elected officials from state and provincial legislatures. . . . And U.S. President George Bush has signed legislation creating the Cascadia Corridor Commission. . . . A disappearing border may be in the cards for the Cascadia region.

In Part I of this book, I referred to the problem presented by hypocrisy in U.S. foreign policy. For example, there was a great outcry when it was learned that the Chinese Communists had financially contributed to American political campaigns. However, the U.S. hypocritically saw nothing wrong with contributing millions of dollars to the political opponents of Yugoslav president Slobodan Milosevic to oust him from office. Specifically concerning Afghanistan, on November 12, 2001, there were reports that the drug-dealing Northern Alliance (U.S. allies) executed, or did not prevent the execution of, at least one hundred supporters of the also drug-dealing Taliban in an area taken by these allies of the U.S. Several months later, Niko Price in Kabul, writing "Mass murder of Taliban alleged" in *The Advertiser* (Adelaide, Australia) on May 4, 2002, stated:

A mass grave of hundreds of men—likely Taliban prisoners killed by their Northern Alliance captors—has been found in northern Afghanistan. The U.S.-based Physicians for Human Rights says interviews with people near Mazar-e-Sharif indicate the men were killed after they surrendered. . . . Dr. Jenny Leaning of the Boston-based group said yesterday Afghan commanders loyal to a variety of groups were operating in the area, as were U.S. troops. "At the time, the U.S. was very active in the air and on the ground," she said. "What did the U.S. know and when and where and what did they do about it?"

Even with claims of war crimes like this, there are serious doubts that any Northern Alliance leaders will be taken before a U.N. war crimes tribunal like the one that now holds Milosevic. And one might also ask what plan American officials had to prevent such atrocities.

Immediately after the terrorist attacks of September 11, President George W. Bush told the nations of the world that they were either with us or against us in the effort against terrorism, but then astonishingly he said what a great ally Communist China was in this effort at about the same time "the Chinese state-run propaganda machine is cashing in on the terror attacks in New York and Washington, producing books, films, and video games glorifying the strikes as a humbling blow against an arrogant nation," according to Damien McElroy in the London *Sunday Telegraph* (November 4). McElroy continued:

Video discs filled with lurid images . . . in the wake of the attacks . . . bear the imprimatur of the Communist Party–controlled media. . . . Communist Party officials say President Jiang Zemin has obsessively watched and re-watched pictures of the aircraft crashing into the World Trade Center. . . . As rescue workers pick through the rubble of the twin towers, the commentator proclaims that the city had reaped the consequences of decades of American bullying of weaker nations. "This is the America the whole world has wanted to see," he said. "Blood debts have been paid in blood. America has bombed other countries and used its hegemony to deny the natural rights of others without paying the price. Who until now has dared to avenge the hurts inflicted by unaccountable Americans."

Do you think there will be a great outcry in Congress to revoke China's Permanent Normal Trade Relations status because of the Chinese government's reaction to the September 11 attack? No, I don't think the power elite would approve of that.

So what should we as a people do? First of all, we should turn back to God. As George Mason, a Founding Father of this nation, stated on August 22, 1787: "By an inevitable chain of causes and effects, Providence punishes national sins by national calamities." God cannot be happy with a nation that condones abortions and other sinful acts. As Second Chronicles 7:14 reads, though, "If my people, which are called by my name, shall humble themselves, and pray, and seek my face, and turn from their wicked ways; then will I hear from heaven, and will forgive their sin, and will heal their land." Then God may once again bless America, for as Matthew 6:33 admonishes us: "But seek ye first the kingdom of God, and his righteousness; and all these things shall be added unto you." Pray steadfastly for America.

Part III

In Part II of this book, "oil" was mentioned as an important part of what has happened in recent months concerning Afghanistan. One of the primary reasons the U.S. and its allies decided to defend Kuwait and Saudi Arabia during the Gulf War a decade ago was to protect the supply of oil coming to the West from those nations. The Gulf War of 1991 was prosecuted for the U.S. by Secretary of Defense Dick Cheney who, upon leaving office in 1993, became CEO of Halliburton, a huge transnational oil services conglomerate.

Because of instability in the Gulf area, major oil corporations began looking more closely at the Caspian Sea area, such as Kazakhstan (which will become the world's largest oil-producing nation, even surpassing Saudi Arabia), and Dick Cheney became a member of the Kazakhstan Oil Advisory Board. Cheney has been a member of the Council on Foreign Relations (CFR), which Prof. Carroll Quigley (Bill Clinton's mentor at Georgetown University) in *Tragedy and Hope* called a "front" group for the power elite. In the CFR's *Foreign Affairs* (May/June 2000) is Michael Klare's "The New Geography of Conflict," in which he remarks that

the region [Central Asia], which stretches from the Ural Moun-

tains to China's western border, has now become a major strategic prize, because of the vast reserves of oil and natural gas
thought to lie under and around the Caspian Sea. Since Central
Command already controls the U.S. forces in the Persian Gulf
region, its assumption of control [taken from Pacific Command
October 1999] over Central Asia means that this area will now
receive close attention from the people whose primary task is to
protect the flow of oil to the United States and its allies.

Not long after the Taliban came to power in Afghanistan, the U.S.
on September 14, 1997, began conducting a joint military exercise
with Kazakhstan just north of Afghanistan. Interestingly, according to the 1952 World Association of Parliamentarians for World
Government map detailing what nations would be policing what
other nations when the world government arrived, American forces
would be in Kazakhstan, Uzbekistan, Tajikistan, Turkmenistan, and
Kirghizstan, which have played an important part in our recent
assault against the Taliban, as the U.S. now has military bases in at
least three of those nations.

Regarding other members of the current Bush presidential
administration who have been connected to the oil industry,
Undersecretary of Commerce Kathleen Cooper was chief econo-
mist for Exxon. And National Security Advisor Condoleezza Rice
for about ten years was on the board of Chevron when it signed a
contract to invest $20 billion over forty years in Kazakhstan. Work-
ing for Rice at the National Security Council was Bush appointee
Zalmay Khalilzad, who was an undersecretary of defense under
former President Bush. Presently, Khalilzad is the current President Bush's special envoy to Afghanistan, even though he had been

a lobbyist for the Taliban. According to a British publication, *The Independent* (October 25, 2001), columnist George Monbiot wrote:

> In 1997, as a paid adviser to the oil multinational UNOCAL, Khalilzad took part in talks with Taliban officials regarding the possibility of building highly lucrative gas and oil pipelines. At the same time, he urged the Clinton administration to take a softer line on the Taliban. By 1997 some of the regime's worst excesses had become public and Mr. bin Laden was ensconced in Afghanistan. That year, the Secretary of State, Madeleine Albright, described the Taliban's abuses of human rights as "despicable." But Mr. Khalilzad defended them in the *Washington Post* ("Afghanistan: Time to Reengage," October 7, 1996): "The Taliban do not practice the anti-U.S. style of fundamentalism practised by Iran. We should . . . be willing to offer recognition and humanitarian assistance and to promote international economic reconstruction."

All of the major oil companies have invested heavily in Kazakhstan and other Caspian area exploration.

Some would argue that the reason we defended Kuwait in the Gulf War was that their people were being killed by Iraqi invaders (U.N. Ambassador Madeleine Albright said, "We think the price was worth it," in response to CBS reporter Leslie Stahl's 1996 question: "We have heard that a half million children have died [as a consequence of our policy against Iraq]. Is the price worth it?"). To that, one might respond that we didn't save about seven hundred thousand Rwandans when they were being slaughtered. Perhaps we would have if there had been oil there, as there was in

Somalia. America and its allies did intervene in the Balkans, though, and it's worth noting that Halliburton's Brown & Root Division received about $180 million to supply U.S. forces there. Halliburton is merging with Dresser Industries, which helped build up the U.S.S.R. years ago. And Skull & Bones member Neil Mallon of Dresser Industries got former President Bush (Skull & Bones member) his first job. On May 28, 1958, attorney and radio commentator Sid Hardin wrote a letter saying Mallon "is under intensive investigation by the U.S. Naval Intelligence, Washington D.C. . . . There is no doubt about it, Mallon is a dangerous operator." (See copy of letter on next page.)

Supposedly, the NATO allies led by the U.S. intervened in the Balkans against Slobodan Milosevic because of ethnic cleansing in Kosovo. However, if ethnic cleansing was the primary concern, why didn't the U.S. intervene in the Sudan where the Muslim government of the north has slaughtered about two million Christians in the south? And if the U.S. is really concerned about ethnic cleansing, why have Dick Cheney and the Bush administration supported the repeal of Section 907 of the 1992 Freedom of Support Act, which restricts U.S. aid to Azerbaijan because of its ethnic cleansing of the Armenians in the Nagomo Karabakh area of Azerbaijan? Could it be because Azerbaijan is very important in obtaining the richest Caspian oil deposits? Could it be that oil was a critical factor in the Kosovo intervention as well? Major western oil corporations had a plan to run a new pipeline from Azerbaijan along the Caspian Sea across the Black Sea through Bulgaria and Kosovo down through Albania to the Adriatic Sea where it could be shipped to the West and around the world. However, Milosevic balked at the plan because it would have siphoned

LAW OFFICER
SID L. HARDIN
SUITES 12-13 FIRST STATE BANK BLDG.
EDINBURG, TEXAS

PLEASE REFER TO FILE NUMBER

May 28, 1958

Dear

Thank you very much for the data received with your letter of May 27th. It is exactly what I need to connect up Judge Hughes with the Dallas Council on World Affairs and similiar anti-anti-communist organizations.

Please send the same data to Judge Joe Greenhill, P. O. Box 1123, Austin, Texas. I talked to Joe a few days ago and he is quite anxious for his campaign manager to have this data. He will deliver the data to his campaign manager, who, in turn will see that it gets to the right places.

I am enclosing herewith copy of our radio script of last Sunday. This particular program created considerable interest and was well received. In fact it stirred up a lot of the Churches, and one Methodist Leader told me he was going to call for an investigation of SMU at the next Texas Conference coming up soon.

I certainly wish we had a radio outlet in either Ft. Worth or Dallas at this time.

Confidentially, H. N. Mallon is under intensive investigation by the U.S. Naval Intelligence, Washington, D.C. Only recently a U.S. Naval Intelligence Officer called on me and photostated my file on Mallon and Dresser Industries and questioned me for two hours and I was unable to answer his questions but obviously Mallon was suspected of some subversive activities or dealings with Russia, and the questions ran all the way from questions about cartels to connections with the Cuban revolt, activities in Venequela, as well as Soviet Espionage Agents. He took my letter from Mallon criticizing my KRLD radio program, but returned it later.

There is no doubt about it, Mallon is a dangerous operator.

Sincerely yours,

Sid L. Hardin

1/slh

off oil from his ally Russia. Not long after this, NATO attacked his forces.

So, did the U.S. cause the recent war against the Taliban in Afghanistan over oil? There is no proof that we caused the war, but we do know the U.S. government has been capable of such activities in the past. In August 1953, CIA director Allen Dulles (who was a CFR president) used a secret $10 million fund to have General Norman Schwarzkopf's father train fighters to overthrow the government of Iran when that nation nationalized its oil production.

The second question is whether the American government was capable of using the September 11 terrorist attack upon the World Trade Center and Pentagon as a pretext for an attack against the Taliban already being considered by the U.S. government. For example, concerning Russia, the *Sydney Morning-Herald* reported March 14, 2000, that a Russian bomb squad officer, Yuri Tkachenko, told Britain's *Observer* newspaper that Russian secret service agents had planted a bomb in a Russian apartment block a week after explosions killed more than 200 people in Moscow. The secret service said it was just a training exercise, but Tkachenko replied: "It was a live bomb," which he had tested and found it was made of Hexagen, the same explosive used in the two Moscow bombs. The *Observer* said his claims threw doubt on Moscow's insistence the bombs were placed by Chechen terrorists. Perhaps Moscow simply needed a "pretext" to take military action against the Chechens.

Concerning the U.S. government, we know that our government has been capable of such things in the past if one looks at Operation Northwoods, presented in a "top secret" document to Secretary of Defense Robert McNamara by the Joint Chiefs of

Staff on March 13, 1962. (See the cover letter for this "top secret" document on the next page.) In this document, the Joint Chiefs suggest pretexts for invading Cuba that would be "suitable for planning purposes," and would be seen as "Cuban provocations" and "camouflage" the fact that the U.S. rather than Cuba caused the events.

For example, the document says that rumors could be started to convince Cubans that an invasion of their island was imminent. This would cause Fidel Castro to attack the U.S. first, and that would serve as a pretext for the American government to invade Cuba. The document also indicates that an American ship could be blown up in Guantanamo Bay, or that a Cuban Communist terror campaign could be developed in the Washington, D.C., area. Another pretext according to the document is that a boatload of Cuban refugees coming to Florida could be sunk, and it also mentions the possibility of hijacking a civilian aircraft and blaming it on the Cubans. Does any of this sound similar to what has happened recently?

The third question is whether it is possible that the U.S. government could have anticipated the September 11 attacks but failed to prevent them. We know that the plan to thwart the 1993 bombing of the World Trade Center was called off by an FBI supervisor (see Ralph Blumenthal's "Tapes Depict Proposal to Thwart Bomb Used in Trade Center Blast," *New York Times,* October 28, 1993). We also know that after the April 19, 1995, Oklahoma City bombing, the police issued an "All Points Bulletin" for "two Mideastern males, 25–28 years of age, six feet tall, athletic build, dark hair and a beard," but the FBI cancelled the APB only hours later. Might these have been among the approximately eight thousand former

~~TOP SECRET SPECIAL HANDLING NOFORN~~

THE JOINT CHIEFS OF STAFF
WASHINGTON 25, D.C.

UNCLASSIFIED   13 March 1962

MEMORANDUM FOR THE SECRETARY OF DEFENSE

Subject: Justification for US Military Intervention
in Cuba (TS)

1. The Joint Chiefs of Staff have considered the attached Memorandum for the Chief of Operations, Cuba Project, which responds to a request of that office for brief but precise description of pretexts which would provide justification for US military intervention in Cuba.

2. The Joint Chiefs of Staff recommend that the proposed memorandum be forwarded as a preliminary submission suitable for planning purposes. It is assumed that there will be similar submissions from other agencies and that these inputs will be used as a basis for developing a time-phased plan. Individual projects can then be considered on a case-by-case basis.

3. Further, it is assumed that a single agency will be given the primary responsibility for developing military and para-military aspects of the basic plan. It is recommended that this responsibility for both overt and covert military operations be assigned the Joint Chiefs of Staff.

For the Joint Chiefs of Staff:

SYSTEMATICALLY REVIEWED
BY JCS ON ___ 21 May 84
CLASSIFICATION CONTINUED

L. L. Lemnitzer

L. L. LEMNITZER
Chairman
Joint Chiefs of Staff

1 Enclosure
Memo for Chief of Operations, Cuba Project   EXCLUDED FROM GDS

> EXCLUDED FROM AUTOMATIC
> REGRADING: DOD DIR 5200.10
> DOES NOT APPLY

~~TOP SECRET SPECIAL HANDLING NOFORN~~

Iraqi soldiers the Clinton administration "resettled" in the U.S. (many in Oklahoma) in 1993–94? Although this "resettlement" occurred during the Clinton administration, the policy was actually established during the previous Bush administration based upon a recommendation by the State Department. It should also be noted that according to investigative reporter Steven Emerson's new book, *American Jihad: The Terrorists Living Among Us,* the radical Muslim group Hamas has been active in Oklahoma City.

In fact, on the very day of the Oklahoma City bombing, "someone other than Tim McVeigh and Terry Nichols 'confessed' to being involved in the terrorist bombing plot that killed 168 people," according to Oklahoma City attorney John M. Johnston in Jon Dougherty's April 18, 2002, *WorldNetDaily* column, "Iraq link to OKC, Sept. 11 attacks?" Dougherty wrote:

> Johnston said Abdul Hakim Murad, who was in federal custody in New York City awaiting trial for plotting to blow up airliners, told jailers . . . "and later the FBI"—that the OKC bombing "had been orchestrated by his former roommate in the Philippines, Ramzi Youssef." . . . Johnston also said his evidence "will show that the Republic of Iraq and [president] Saddam Hussein were involved in funding and planning" the OKC bombing. . . . The Oklahoma attorney, in his statement, claims that "certain elements of the United States government must have known" about the "foreign involvement all along."

Further along these lines, on November 17, 1999, the U.S. District Court of Western Oklahoma filed an order for Case 97-1535-L that stated:

... The court accepts as undisputed the following facts as stated by defendants. .... On April 20, 1995, federal authorities detained Abraham Abdallah Ahmad, a Jordanian-American resident of Oklahoma City, in London, England, as a possible witness in the bombing. Ahmad was reported to have duffel bags containing electrical tape, silicone, a hammer, tweezers, and a photo album with pictures of missiles and other weapons. Ahmad was reported to have left his home in northwest Oklahoma City approximately a half hour after the bombing and flown to Chicago, then London en route to Jordan. ...

Instead of pursuing a Middle Eastern connection to the Oklahoma City bombing of April 19, 1995, federal authorities seemed intent upon blaming only Timothy McVeigh and Terry Nichols. However, in the "Washington Whispers" section of *U.S. News & World Report* (October 29, 2001), one finds that

a few top Defense officials think Oklahoma City bomber Timothy McVeigh was an Iraqi agent. The theory stems from a never-before-reported allegation that McVeigh had allegedly collected Iraqi telephone numbers. Why haven't we heard this before about the case of the executed McVeigh? Conspiracy theorists in the Pentagon think it's part of a cover-up.

In addition to McVeigh perhaps being an Iraqi agent, Kelly Patricia O'Meara in "Iraq Connections to U.S. Extremists" (*Insight Magazine,* December 3, 2001) wrote of the connection of Terry Nichols to elements of Iraqi intelligence. She stated:

Nichols reportedly attended a meeting in the early 1990s on the predominantly Muslim island of Mindanao, a hotbed of fundamentalist activities, at which Ramzi Yousef (mastermind of the World Trade Center bombing of 1993), Abdul Hakim Murad and Wali Khan Amin Shah were present. The themes of the meetings were "bombing activities, providing firearms and ammunition, training in making and handling bombs."

O'Meara then related information from an interview with Laurie Mylroie, a Harvard-trained Ph.D. expert on Iraqi terrorism, in which Mylroie remarked:

> I doubt that Nichols has ever been asked about his connections to Yousef because the [U.S.] government didn't want to know. It wanted to say, "Here are the perpetrators; we arrested them and we brought them to justice. Case closed." . . . The kind of irresponsibility that I and others believe the Clinton administration committed is so mind-boggling that many well-meaning people just can't believe it, even though there is significant evidence—a standard of probable cause. They find it hard to accept because it would follow that the White House and the FBI were corrupt.

O'Meara later in the article referred to an Iraqi's "commentary on biological warfare and . . . the progress of the Iraqi program in the United States." In Kenneth Timmerman's article "Iraqi Connection to Oklahoma Bombing," posted March 25, 2002, in *Insight Magazine,* one finds out that

the facts [Oklahoma City attorney Mike] Johnston and his team
of investigators uncovered could blow the lid off the U.S. government cover-up of the "others unknown" who conspired with
Timothy McVeigh and Terry Nichols to murder 168 Americans. . . . The government was withholding evidence, as Department of Justice Inspector General Glenn A. Fine admitted
in an official report released on March 18.

Two days after the September 11, 2001, attack upon the World Trade
Center and Pentagon, attorney David Schippers (chief investigative counsel for the U.S. House Judiciary Committee during the
Clinton impeachment process) was on WRRK radio in Pittsburgh
and said that six weeks before September 11, he had tried to warn
U.S. Attorney-General John Ashcroft that he (Schippers) had received information from FBI agents and others that a terrorist attack was being planned for lower Manhattan. Schippers indicated
that lower level Justice Department officials blocked him from
getting the information to Ashcroft.

Two months later, in the *Indianapolis Star* (November 17, 2001),
James Patterson in "Missing Evidence from Oklahoma City," wrote:

The FBI doesn't want to talk about it, but the evidence keeps
mounting. Critical evidence that several Middle Eastern men
may have been connected to the Oklahoma City bombing ap-
pears to have been kept from the public by the FBI. At a mini-
mum, Congress should question one former FBI agent who
says he obtained 22 affidavits and more than 30 witness statements describing sightings of Middle Easterners with McVeigh.
Although he passed the materials on to a superior, the evidence

never surfaced and was not given to McVeigh's or Nichols' defense teams. . . . The [FBI] agents believe if that evidence had not been suppressed by the FBI, it could have helped uncover plans leading to the September 11 attacks on the World Trade Center and Pentagon. Lawmakers should demand a full accounting of the missing documents given to the FBI. . . . In 1999, the agent got the documents from former Oklahoma City KFOR-TV reporter Jayna Davis. Davis had done a six-year investigation beginning on the day of the bombing, documenting a cell of Middle Eastern individuals operating in Oklahoma City under suspicious circumstances. "She started in 1997 trying to turn those documents over to the FBI and we refused to take those documents because we knew at the time that those documents would have to be turned over to the defense attorneys, . . ." said the former agent. Two weeks ago, the Justice Department quashed motions to allow 18 FBI agents, including the agent who received the documents from Davis, to testify in Nichols' state case. At least one of those agents believes that if the FBI had followed up on the affidavits that he turned over to his superiors, the September 11 attacks could have been prevented. "We don't know whatever happened to those documents," the former agent said. . . . "We did have some Oklahoma connections to the events in Washington, D.C., and New York City. We did find out that one of these individuals was trying to take flight training at a Norman [Oklahoma] flight instruction school."

Is it possible the government today is covering up information relevant to September 11? Relevant to this, we know that the government has not been forthcoming about the terrorist connection to the downing of TWA 800, because in Yossef Bodansky's *Bin Laden* (1999), this director of the U.S. House of Representatives Task Force on Terrorism and Unconventional Warfare stated:

> In the early months of 1996 Tehran started laying the foundations for the next phase in the terrorist *jihad,* establishment of the HizbAllah International, with bin Laden in a senior position. The significance of this organization for the prevailing terrorist threat was demonstrated in its first strikes: the bombing of the U.S. barracks in Khobar, Saudi Arabia; the downing of TWA 800; and the assassination of a U.S. intelligence officer in Cairo. The Iranians now clearly acknowledged not only the importance of the "Afghans" and other Sunni Islamist radicals but also the distinction of their chosen leaders—specifically bin Laden and Zawahiri.

Further relevant to Iran, in the *Deutsche Presse-Agentur* article, "Reports of Attempts to Warn U.S. of Impending Attacks" (September 14, 2001), one learns that in the German newspaper *Neue Presse,* there was a report of an Iranian man being held by German police, who allowed him to call the U.S. Secret Service to tell them of an attack that would take place the week of September 10, 2001, but American officials discontinued the call when he told them he was waiting to be deported from Germany. The 29-year-old also just hours before the September 11 attacks tried to fax a letter to President Bush but was not allowed to do so.

A BBC "Newsnight" segment November 6, 2001, began with the question, "Has someone been sitting on the FBI?" In the segment, Joe Trento (author of *Secret History of the CIA*) says, "The sad thing [about September 11] is that thousands of Americans had to die needlessly." The segment then referred to an FBI "secret" case ID: 199-Eye WF213 589, which was an investigation of Osama bin Laden's younger brother, Abdullah bin Laden, president of World Assembly of Muslim Youth (WAMY) at 5613 Leesburg Pike, Falls Church, Virginia, and four of the hijackers of September 11 lived nearby at 5913 Leesburg Pike. The BBC segment then noted that the U.S. Treasury had *not* frozen the assets of WAMY, and Joe Trento said the FBI was pulled off the investigation. The BBC segment next included an interview with Michael Springman, who was head of the American visa bureau in Jeddah, Saudi Arabia. He said the State Department years ago had him issue visas for Osama bin Laden's recruits, and they came to the U.S. for terrorist training by the CIA against the Soviets. Then the BBC segment contained an interview with Michael Wildes, who represented a Saudi Arabian diplomat who defected to the U.S. with fourteen thousand documents implicating Saudis in financing terrorism, and the FBI men to whom he showed the documents told him they were not permitted to read all of them.

Why the hands-off approach toward Muslims in the U.S.? For some time now, American society has been told not to offend those of other faiths, and that we should "respect" all religions. For example, the Newark, New Jersey, *Star-Ledger* (March 18, 1983) reported that Archbishop Jean Jadot, president of the Vatican Secretariat for Non-Christians, "is expected to urge Catholics to deepen their Christian faith through respect for the spirituality of all the world's religions. Citing Hindu, Islamic, Buddhist and Chinese religious traditions. Archbishop Jadot will urge pastors . . . to regard the members of these religions as 'believers.'" Perhaps this is why on May 14, 1999, Pope John Paul II kissed the Koran. And even more recently, a course is being taught today at Excelsior public middle school near Oakland, in which one hundred twenty-five seventh graders dress in Muslim robes, adopt Muslim names, and act out pilgrimages to Mecca. The school superintendent said they are simply following California's state-mandated standards.

One individual who did not take a hands-off approach to investigating radical Muslims was John O'Neill, an FBI agent who for years led U.S. investigations into Osama bin Laden and the al-Qaeda network of terrorists. In the *Irish Times* article, "U.S. efforts to make peace summed up by 'oil'" (November 19, 2001), is a look at *Bin Laden: The Forbidden Truth* by Jean-Charles Brisard (who wrote a 1997 report an al-Qaeda for the French secret services) and Guillaume Dasquie. The article indicated that the book is "a tribute to O'Neill," and that Brisard said O'Neill "complained bitterly that the U.S. State Department—and behind it the oil lobby who make up President Bush's entourage—blocked attempts to prove bin Laden's guilt. . . . In August 2001, O'Neill resigned in frustration and took up a new job as head of security at the World Trade Center. He died in the September 11 attack." The article went on to tell how Laila Helms (part-Afghan niece of former CIA director Richard Helms), described as the Mata Hari of the U.S.-Taliban negotiations, brought Sayed Hashimi (advisor to Mullah Omar) to meet with CIA and State Department officials in March 2001.

In a related article by Julio Godoy in Paris for the *Inter Press Service* (November 15, 2001), Brisard is quoted as saying: "At one moment during the negotiations, the U.S. representatives told the

Taliban, 'either you accept our offer of a carpet of gold, or we bury you under a carpet of bombs.'"

Why would the U.S. offer the Taliban "a carpet of gold"? In *The Grand Chessboard* (1997), Zbigniew Brzezinski (CFR member, first director of the Trilateral Commission, and President Jimmy Carter's national security advisor) referred several times to "ruling national elites," and stated that "for the United States, Eurasian geostrategy involves the purposeful management of geostrategically dynamic states. . . . Azerbaijan . . . can be described as the vitally important 'cork' controlling access to the 'bottle' that contains the [oil, gas, and mineral] riches of the Caspian Sea basin and Central Asia." Brzezinski then described the importance not only of a pipeline crossing the Caspian Sea to Azerbaijan, but also one going to the Arabian Sea through Afghanistan. He explained

> that America's primary interest is to help ensure that no single power comes to control this geopolitical space [Eurasia] and that the global community has unhindered financial and economic access to it. . . . America is now Eurasia's arbiter. . . . How the United States both manipulates and manages Eurasia's key geopolitical pivots will be critical to the longevity and stability of America's global primacy. . . . As in chess, American global planners must think several moves ahead. . . . In the course of the next several decades, a functioning structure of global cooperation . . . could emerge and gradually assume the mantle of the world's current "regent."

Relevant to recent events, Brzezinski wrote: "A possible challenge to American primacy from Islamic fundamentalism could be part of the problem in this unstable region . . . and would be likely to express itself through diffuse violence." And relevant to American power and recent events, he wrote:

> The pursuit of power is not a goal that commands popular passion, except in conditions of a sudden threat or challenge to the public's sense of domestic well-being. . . . America may find it more difficult to fashion a consensus on foreign policy issues, except in the circumstances of a truly massive and widely perceived direct external threat.

The *Inter Press Service* article by Julio Godoy mentioned earlier indicated that Niaz Naik, former Pakistani minister for foreign affairs, said that at a meeting in Berlin in July 2001, Tom Simons, the U.S. representative, openly threatened the Taliban and Pakistan: "Simons said, 'either the Taliban behave as they ought to, or Pakistan convinces them to do so, or we shall use another option.' The words Simons used were 'a military operation,'" Naik claimed.

Further along these lines, *The Guardian* (London) on September 22, 2001, reported that Simons (former U.S. ambassador to Pakistan) was accompanied at the Berlin meeting by Karl "Rick" Inderfurth (a former assistant secretary of state for South Asian Affairs) and Lee Coldren (Rhodes scholar who headed the office of Pakistan, Afghan, and Bangladesh Affairs in the State Department until 1997). The article went on to indicate that these three people

> were no longer government officials but had close links with their governments. . . . Asked whether he could be sure that the

Americans were passing ideas from the Bush administration rather than their own views, Mr. Naik said yesterday: "What the Americans indicated to us was perhaps based on official instructions. They were very senior people." . . . Mr. Coldren confirmed the broad outline of the American position at the Berlin meeting yesterday. "I think there was some discussion of the fact that the United States was so disgusted with the Taliban that they might be considering some military action." The three former U.S. diplomats "based our discussion on hearsay from U.S. officials," he said. . . . Mr. Simons [said], "We were clear that feeling in Washington was strong, and that military action was one of the options down the road. . . ."

Perhaps this is why one reads in Lawrence Wright's "The Counter-Terrorist" (*New Yorker,* January 14, 2002) about John O'Neill that Richard Clarke, the national coordinator for counter-terrorism in the White House, "on July 5, 2001, summoned all the domestic security agencies—the Federal Aviation Administration, the Coast Guard, Customs, the Immigration and Naturalization Service, and the FBI—and told them to increase their security in light of an impending attack."

According to Barton Gellman's article, "Before Sept. 11, Unshared Clues and Unshaped Policy," in the *Washington Post* (May 17, 2002), Clarke said: "Something really spectacular is going to happen here, and it's going to happen soon." Gellman went on to write:

Director of Central Intelligence George J. Tenet had been "nearly frantic" with concern since June 22, according to one frequent interlocutor, and a written intelligence summary for national security adviser Condoleezza Rice said on June 28: "It is highly likely that a significant al-Qaeda attack is in the near future, within several weeks."

Did we expect an attack against the U.S. because we had threatened military action against the Taliban? Does any of this sound like the 1962 Joint Chiefs of Staff document regarding rumors of invasion of Cuba, possibly causing the Cubans to attack the U.S., giving the American government the pretext it needed for invading Cuba?

The question then is, "What did our government know and when did it know it?" The *New Yorker* article mentioned above indicated that ABC news reporter John Miller's narration of his spring 1998 interview with Osama bin Laden "contained information to the effect that one of bin Laden's aides was cooperating with the FBI." The article also indicated that "a member of al-Qaeda had walked into the American Embassy in Nairobi and told the CIA of the bombing plot" against the embassy before it occurred in August 1998. Moreover, in the new book *American Jihad: The Terrorists Living Among Us* by Steven Emerson (national security correspondent for *U.S. News & World Report* from 1986 to 1990, and producer of the 1994 program "Jihad in America" on PBS), there is a chart showing "Current and Recent Militant Islamist Groups in the U.S.," with al-Qaeda listed as being in Boston, Denver, Tucson, and Orlando among other cities, Hamas listed as having both groups and conventions in Oklahoma City, and Islamic Jihad listed as being in Cleveland, Tampa, and Raleigh, North Carolina, among other cities. When the NBC affiliate in Raleigh called the FBI and asked who and where the Islamic Jihad were there, the affiliate was told by the FBI that they would not say where and who they are. This seems somewhat curious, given that since September 11, Homeland Security Chief Tom Ridge and U.S. Attorney-General John Ashcroft have more than once advised all Americans to be on "high alert" for terrorist activities.

Again, one might ask, "What did our government know and when did it know it?" David S. Cloud and Jeanne Cummings, writing "Bush Discloses Terror-Report Details" for the *Wall Street Journal* (May 17, 2002), revealed:

> White House officials said that on August 6, 2001, while on vacation at his Texas ranch, Mr. Bush received a one-and-a-half page summary of al-Qaeda terrorist threats. In the report, air-liner hijacking was mentioned twice as a possible tactic. . . . Mr. Bush's briefing coincided with rising concern at the Central Intelligence Agency that Mr. bin Laden was planning to strike not overseas, but on U.S. soil. In early August, the agency cir-culated a classified intelligence report that concluded Mr. bin Laden was determined to strike inside the U.S., officials said. . . . The Federal Bureau of Investigation recently disclosed it received a memo from its Phoenix field office warning that Ar-abs were seeking pilot, security, and airport-operations training in the U.S., and they might be part of a terrorist plot.

Furthermore, according to *Frankfurter Allgemeine Zeitung* (Septem-ber 14, 2001), the BND (German intelligence) warned the CIA and Israel before September 11 that Middle Eastern terrorists were "planning to hijack commercial aircraft to use as weapons to attack important symbols of American and Israeli culture." Shortly there-after, *The Times of India* (October 9) in Manoj Joshi's article, "India helped FBI trace ISI-terrorist links," revealed that General Mahmud Ahmad (former director-general of Pakistan's intelligence service [ISI]) had Ahmad Umar Sheikh wire $100,000 to hijacker Mohammed Atta. General Ahmad arrived in the U.S. on September 4, and stayed after September 11 talking to officials at the CIA and Pentagon before the September 11 attacks and to officials at the State Department after the attacks. Might he have communicated with hijack leader Atta before the attack? One should also remember here that General Ahmad was a "U.S. approved appointee" as head of the ISI, because throughout the post-Cold War era till the present, Pakistan was the launching pad for CIA covert operations in the Caucusus, Central Asia, and the Balkans. In October 2001, Michael Chossudovsky of the Centre for Research on Globalisation indicated that "on the 9th of September while General Ahmad was in the U.S., the leader of the Northern Alliance, Commander Ahmad Shah Masood, was assassinated. The Northern Alliance had informed the Bush Administration that the ISI was allegedly implicated in the assassination."

One might also reasonably ask how Ali Mohammed could train Green Berets, then work for the CIA before working for the FBI in Sacramento from 1992 to 1996, and yet the U.S. government knew nothing of his involvement in the bombing of the World Trade Center and the American embassies in Kenya and Tanzania before they occurred. He was indicted in New York on those charges in 1998.

Jack Kelley in "Saudi Money Aiding bin Laden: Businessmen are financing front groups" (*USA Today*, October 29, 2001) noted that the U.S. and Britain were investigating Capitol Trust Bank of New York and London for allegedly transferring millions of dollars to Osama bin Laden from five prominent Saudi Arabian businessmen. The bank is headed by Mohammed Alamoudi, whose lawyer in Washington, D.C., has been Vernon Jordan, a friend of Bill Clinton and CFR member.

Relevant to the Clinton years, Steven Emerson in the March 13, 1996, edition of the *Wall Street Journal* wrote "Friends of Hamas in the White House," in which he revealed that Bill and Hillary Clinton embraced an Islamic group, the America Muslim Council, that supports Hamas. On November 9, 1995, President Clinton and Vice-President Al Gore met with Abdulrahman Alamoudi, executive director of the American Muslim Council, which supports Islamic terrorists, according to Seif Ashmawy (American Muslim publisher of the *Voice of Peace* in New Jersey). Emerson wrote that Abdulrahman Alamoudi

> emerged as the primary defender of Musa Abu Marzuq, the Hamas political bureau chief responsible for creating the group's death squads, whose handiwork was seen in the last three weeks in Israel. . . . (Curiously, even as federal investigators had begun making headway last fall in identifying U.S. terrorist front groups, federal counter-terrorism officials say that the recommendations were shelved at the White House.)

Emerson followed this article with another in the August 5, 1996, *Wall Street Journal* titled "Stop Aid and Comfort for Patrons of Terror," in which he described the activities of a University of South Florida professor named Sami Al-Arian, who was at the time under federal investigation for organizing a series of conferences which featured a number of the world's top terrorist leaders. Given this information, why then in July 2000 in Tampa did George W. Bush and his wife Laura have their photos taken with the Al-Arian family, and presidential candidate Bush during a campaign speech there singled out Al-Arian's son, Abdullah, positively calling him "Big Dude"? A *Geostrategy-Direct Intelligence Brief* titled "U.S. covering up Saudi terror support?" was posted on *WorldNetDaily* on May 9, 2002. It referred to a lawsuit filed in a Florida court by former U.S. prosecutor John Loftus, who said the State Department asked the Justice Department to terminate a 1995 criminal investigation of Sami Al-Arian after the discovery of Saudi involvement. According to the *WorldNetDaily* brief, "the reason for the hands-off approach, Loftus said, is that prosecution of Al-Arian would disclose that he was a 'small, but significant part of a global money laundering network operated under the guise of purported American charities run by the government of Saudi Arabia.'"

On September 11, 2001 (exactly ten years to the day since former President Bush gave his "New World Order" speech to the U.N.), terrorists attacked the World Trade Center and the Pentagon. Two days later, on September 13, Associated Newspapers, Ltd., published Keith Dovkants' article, "CIA comes under fire for lapses," in which he reported that the FBI and CIA and Joint Terrorist Task Force had known that Osama bin Laden had set his sights on destroying the World Trade Center. Dovkants also wrote:

> In France, the counterespionage agency, the DST, appears to
> have had reports that an attack on American interests in France
> was being planned by the bin Laden network. The French iden-

tified a man arrested by the FBI as an Islamic activist involved in the Pakistan-Afghan orbit and were astonished to hear nothing back.

Offering something of a defense for the CIA, one of its former top field officers, Robert Baer, at a luncheon of Accuracy in Media on May 16, 2002, said the Clinton administration "dismantled the CIA. The CIA has no sources in Saudi Arabia. None. They closed their eyes. Too risky. We must not offend the Saudis. They control 25% of the world's oil. There was not a single Mosque-watcher when clerics were recruiting people" for Osama bin Laden's al-Qaeda network. Baer said the situation went back to the 1970s when the U.S. "cut a deal with Saudi Arabia saying: 'You invest your money and buy our arms, and we'll take your oil. No questions asked.'"

Of course, it's not just the FBI and CIA which have come under criticism, but the Immigration and Naturalization Service (INS) as well. Relevant to the INS and its problems, *Jewish World Review* (November 14, 2001) published Michelle Malkin's "An INS horror story" about Walter D. Cadman, who had become INS district director in Miami in 1992. Malkin said that in June 1995, Cadman participated in an elaborate scheme to deceive a congressional fact-finding delegation, but even so, in 1998 he was quietly named head of the INS' National Security Unit, where he coordinates anti-terrorism efforts. How secure from terrorists should that make us feel? Furthermore, what does it say about the INS that it granted a student visa to hijacker Mohammed Atta on July 17, 2001, and to hijacker Marwan al-Shehhi on August 9, 2001, and the flight school where they trained received notice of the approval of these student visas on March 11, 2002, exactly six months after the September 11, 2001, attacks? If the INS is this careless, might it today be granting visas to other terrorists?

After the attack on September 11, the U.S. government gave an ultimatum to the Taliban in Afghanistan to turn over Osama bin Laden and the al-Qaeda network or face military action. Many were surprised when the Taliban chose to confront American military might, but should they have been surprised, given what the U.S. government itself had been supporting in that country? The *Washington Post* (March 23, 2002) front-page article, "From U.S., the ABCs of Jihad," begins with the following words:

> In the twilight of the Cold War, the United States spent millions of dollars to supply Afghan schoolchildren with textbooks filled with violent images and militant Islamic teachings. . . . The primers, which were filled with talk of *jihad* and featured drawings of guns, bullets, soldiers, and mines, have served since then as the Afghan school system's core curriculum. . . . The textbooks were developed in the early 1980s under an AID [U.S. Agency for International Development] grant to the University of Nebraska-Omaha and its Center for Afghanistan Studies. . . . During that time of Soviet occupation . . . in Afghanistan . . . [AID] agency officials . . . acknowledged that at the time it also suited U.S. interests to stoke hatred of foreign invaders. . . . The textbooks continued to circulate in various versions, even after the Taliban seized power in 1996. . . . Today, the books remain widely available in schools and shops. . . . There is a Pashtu tribute to the *mujaheddin,* who are described as obedient to Allah. Such men will sacrifice their wealth and life itself to impose Islamic law on the government, the text says. . . . In

early January, UNICEF began printing new texts for many subjects but arranged to supply copies of the old, unrevised U.S.
books for other subjects, including Islamic instruction. Within
days, the Afghan interim government announced that it would
use the old AID-produced texts for its core curriculum."

Why should anyone be surprised that many Afghan Muslim youth
educated with these texts in the 1980s as adults in 2001 would be
willing to "sacrifice their life" resisting American "foreign invaders"?

When the U.S. recently took military action against the Taliban
for harboring bin Laden and his al-Qaeda terrorists in Afghanistan, the American government supported the Northern Alliance
in that country against the Taliban. The Northern Alliance has been
sustained by Moscow since 1990, however, and despite U.S. ob-
jections, the Northern Alliance (with Russian support) entered
Kabul before a new Afghan government was formed. Thus, the
Russians now have a stronghold in Afghanistan.

Another American "ally" in the war against terrorism is China,
but how do we know the Chinese Communists will not sneak
small nuclear devices into the U.S. via COSCO (China Ocean
Shipping Co.), which is trying to buy a new container facility in
Tampa, Florida (where the U.S. Central Command headquarters
is located)? They wouldn't even need an ICBM capability then!
How can we overlook this type of potential Chinese threat? Not
only was Nancy Dorn (registered foreign agent for the Chinese-
controlled Hutchison-Whampoa) national security advisor to GOP
House Speaker Dennis Hastert, but on December 19, 2001, she
was nominated as President Bush's Office of Management and

Budget deputy director.

When the U.S. was psychologically preparing the American people for the military war against Afghanistan, Americans were shown photos of how the ruling Taliban cut off the hands of robbers, and women who committed adultery were killed. Laura Bush and other American women were outraged at this, and so with the defeat of the Taliban, the Bush administration supports Hamid Karzai as Afghanistan's interim chairman, and Karzai has said that Islamic law will be strictly enforced there, and "thieves will have their hands cut off and adulterers [women only] will be stoned [to death]." Have you heard Laura Bush condemn these remarks? And most of the American media has remained largely silent about Karzai's remarks, as loyal members of the power elite might be expected to do.

Interestingly, Karzai was a consultant for UNOCAL oil corporation during the planning of the proposed Afghani pipeline which the Taliban was resisting. Also of relevant interest is the fact that on February 12, 1998, UNOCAL vice-president of international relations, John J. Maresca (former minister in the U.S. embassy in France and ambassador to the Organization for Security and Cooperation in Europe, who would become a special ambassador to Afghanistan) testified before the U.S. House of Representatives Subcommittee on Asia and the Pacific of the Committee on International Relations, saying the following:

> From the outset, we have made it clear that construction of the [oil] pipeline we have proposed across Afghanistan could not begin until a recognized government is in place that has the confidence of governments, lenders, and our company. . . . Last

October, the Central Asia Gas Pipeline Consortium, called CentGas, in which UNOCAL holds an interest, was formed to develop a gas pipeline. . . . As with the proposed Central Asia oil pipeline, CentGas cannot begin construction until an internationally recognized Afghanistan government is in place. . . . The impact of these resources on U.S. commercial interests and U.S. foreign policy is also significant.

Another reason the American public was eager to support military efforts against the terrorists was that anthrax was discovered in several locations and killed a few Americans. Interestingly, BioPort is the only corporation in the U.S. licensed to make an anthrax vaccine, and one of its major customers is the Department of Defense. Curiously, it was determined some weeks after the anthrax exposures in the U.S. that this particular strain came not from Iraq or Russia, but rather it was the same strain that is at Fort Detrick, Maryland, which, of course, is under the Department of Defense. Investors in BioPort have included the Carlyle Group, for which former President Bush is a consultant and marketer, and the current President Bush has received fees as director of a subsidiary of Carlyle Corporation. Also noteworthy is the fact that the bin Laden family had investments in Carlyle until just after September 11.

Recently, President Bush referred to the "axis of evil," meaning North Korea, Iran, and Iraq. Talk show host John Loeffler has questioned why Bush didn't include Cuba in the axis, given the information in former Castro senior diplomat Juan Benemelis' two articles in *Cuba: Assessing the Threat to U.S. Security,* edited by Adolfo Leyva de Varona. The articles detail Castro's support for terrorist activities (including those by radical Muslims) around the world.

There are those in the current Bush administration who would like to finish the effort against Saddam Hussein begun by former President Bush. And in that regard, on February 2, 2002, in Munich, United States officials called upon NATO to transform their military union into a terrorism-fighting alliance and consider Iraq their first target. Deputy Secretary of Defense Paul Wolfowitz and Senator John McCain urged NATO allies to join in an effort against Iraq, but said the U.S. would act alone if necessary. Senator Joseph Lieberman agreed with Sen. McCain, who said, "A terrorist resides in Baghdad. . . . A day of reckoning is approaching." Four hundred invited attendees at Munich were taken aback by the comments, and a member of the British Parliament said there would have to be incontrovertible proof that Iraq had engaged in terrorism. So concerned about a possible attack by the U.S. against Iraq was German chancellor Gerhard Schroeder that he asked President Bush about it, and the Associated Press in Berlin on February 10 reported that Bush assured Schroeder the U.S. has no intention of attacking Iraq. Of course, if these threats of an attack caused Iraq to take some action against the U.S. or an American, might that serve as a pretext for an American attack against Iraq (remember the 1962 Joint Chiefs of Staff document)?

Remember from Part I of this book that the power elite is primarily interested in using the reaction (e.g., public willingness to sacrifice some freedoms for safety) to an action (e.g., terrorist attack) to further their globalist goals. As noted earlier, on the afternoon of September 11, 2001, ABC News/*Washington Post* released poll results showing that at least two-thirds of those surveyed "would sacrifice some personal liberties in support of anti-terrorism efforts." This sentiment even increased over time, as on the March 8, 2002, edition of ABC's "Nightline," titled "Home-land Security: At Any Cost," the following statements occurred at the beginning of the broadcast. Host Ted Koppel stated: "When national security is at stake, we have to be prepared to make adjustments. We're going to have to sacrifice some of our personal liberties." He then played a tape of President Bush saying, "We will pay whatever price it takes to defend America." And then Koppel remarked, "The question is, 'How far are we willing to go?' . . . A recent national poll asked, 'Will Americans have to give up some freedoms to make the country safe?' And 79 percent said, 'Yes.'"

Relevant to recent events and the loss of some personal freedoms, Associated Press special correspondent Charles J. Hanley's article "Big Brother Returns" (*Santa Cruz Sentinel,* January 14, 2002) stated:

In parliament chambers and cabinet rooms around the globe, the fears and suspicions of a world on edge are fast translating into the cold legal language of police power. . . . In Russia, Spain, India and elsewhere as well, some foresee the anti-terror offensive being turned into a campaign against political dissent. Government leaders counter that if they are to head off terror attacks, they have no choice but to equip police and intelligence agencies with new authority to eavesdrop, to dip into private files, to lock away people on mere suspicions. . . . Through legislation and presidential order, the U.S. government has resorted to secret detentions of hundreds of people, to loosened rules on wiretapping, to listening in on lawyer-client conversations, to contemplating closed military tribunals for terrorism suspects.

... In Berlin the debate was muted as the German Parliament gave police authority to seek information on individuals from financial institutions, telecommunications companies and airlines—all previously prohibited. The government also gained the power to outlaw religious organizations for promoting ideals that could be linked to terrorism.

The title given to this article by Hanley seems most appropriate, as all of the things mentioned in it will be necessary for the accomplishment of the power elite's global control.

The power elite has been psychologically preparing the American public for global control for many years. In the National Education Association (NEA) Yearbook for 1937, one finds the following:

The present capitalist and nationalist school system has been supplanted in but one place—Russia—and that change was affected by revolution. Hence the verdict of history would seem to indicate that we are likely to have to depend upon revolution for social change of an important and far-reaching character.

Then, as the Second World War ended, the editor of the *NEA Journal* wrote an article in its January 1946 edition titled "The Teacher and World Government," in which editor Joy Elmer Morgan stated: "In the struggle to establish an adequate world government, the teacher . . . can do much to prepare the hearts and minds of children for global understanding and cooperation." This psychological preparation and conditioning was continued by NEA official William Carr in the October 1947 edition of the same journal, in which he advocated that teachers "teach about the various proposals that have been made for strengthening the United Nations and the establishment of world law. Teach those attitudes which will result ultimately in the creation of a world citizenship and world government." (The concept of world citizenship will be reaffirmed in a publication, "World Citizenship: A Global Ethic for Sustainable Development," by the Baha'i International Community in the 1990s.)

In the April 1949 edition of *United Nations World,* Ambassador Warren Austin, chief of the U.S. Mission to the U.N., wrote:

> We must look far ahead to our final goal of world peace under law: that introduces World Federation. . . . World Government . . . could not be accepted without radical change of national outlook. . . . It will take a long time to prepare peoples and governments of most nations for acceptance of and participation in a world government. . . . If we expect this future world government to be created by agreement and not by force or conquest, we will have to be willing to work patiently until peoples or governments are ready for it.

And in an effort to "make peoples ready for it," exactly fifty years ago in the 1952 edition of F. A. Magruder's textbook, *American Government,* one reads:

> When we have definite international laws and an army to enforce them, we shall have international peace. When atomic bombs are made only by a world government and used only by a world army, who could resist? . . . Give the U.N. absolute

power to regulate international trade and commerce. . . . Immigration control now handled by each country would be relinquished to the U.N. along with the power to arbitrarily remove people from one part of the world and settle them in a place a U.N. planner determines their skills, etc., are needed. . . . Establish an international police force strong enough that no nation can resist its orders. . . . Give the U.N. power of taxation. . . . Place control of broadcast stations, press, speech, etc., under U.N. control to insure development of "cooperative" public opinion.

Hasn't much of this been in the process of coming to pass in recent years?

And speaking of recent years, in the World Federalist Association's 1994 document "The Genius of Federation: Why World Federation Is the Answer to Global Problems," one can see the globalists' strategy revealed, when one reads:

> Still another approach is to advance step by step toward global governance, using the U.N. but without trying to amend the Charter. Let the U.N. establish new agencies such as an International Criminal Court (which can try individuals for violations of international law) or a U.N. Arms Control and Disarmament Agency (which can set up a program for arms reduction with verification capabilities and punishments for individuals who try to defy it). . . . By means of these voluntarily funded functional agencies national sovereignty would be gradually eroded until it is no longer an issue. Eventually a world federation can be formally adopted with little resistance.

The only question is whether the public will wake up to the power elite's machinations and have the will to actively resist their plans for global control. We must continue to pray for America.

Other important events in 2001 relevant to the terrorist attacks of September 11:

- June: testimony in the millennium bombing plot trial indicates that al-Qaeda may attack the U.S.
- July 5: Phoenix FBI agent Kenneth Williams urges an investigation of Middle Eastern men at U.S. flight training schools to see if they might be part of an al-Qaeda plot. Phoenix supervisor Bill Kurtz sends the report to FBI headquarters, but officials there delay action.
- Late July: FAA issues warnings that terrorists may be training for hijackings.
- August 6: CIA briefs President Bush that al-Qaeda may hijack airplanes.
- Mid-August: Zacarias Moussaoui is arrested by FBI after tip from Minneapolis flight school. An FBI agent in Minneapolis warns that Moussaoui might be planning to "fly something into the World Trade Center."

After all of these and other events, why did FBI director Robert Mueller on September 17, 2001, tell reporters that "there was no warning signs that I'm aware of that would indicate this type of operation in the country"? And why did President George Bush on December 21, 2001, tell reporters that "America never dreamt before September the 11th anybody would attack us"?

Part IV

September 11 was one of many steps leading us toward the New World Order, and those steps began over two hundred years ago with the Illuminati. Many people do not believe the tremendous influence which the Illuminati has had on history, but there is ample evidence, for example, in "Transactions of the Quator Coronati Lodge" (or the Ars Quator Coronatorum) that by the mid-1790s, Napoleon had been initiated into the Illuminati via French Freemasonic lodges under its control. Another individual, the Marquis de Luchet, who had also been initiated into the French Grand Orient lodges controlled by the Illuminati, distributed early in 1789 (prior to the French Revolution) a pamphlet which he wrote and which stated:

> Deluded people, learn that there exists a conspiracy in favor of despotism, against liberty, of incapacity against talent, of vice against virtue, of ignorance against enlightenment. This society aims at governing the world. Its object is universal domination. This plan may seem extraordinary, incredible, yes, but not chimeral. No such calamity has ever yet afflicted the world.

In the United States, President George Washington's secretary of state, Thomas Jefferson, was not an outspoken critic of the Illuminati or its founder, Adam Weishaupt. In fact, Jefferson tried to persuade Washington not to come out publicly against the democratic societies that fomented the Whiskey Rebellion in western Pennsylvania. The rebellion was caused mainly by the Mingo Creek Democratic Society, established by an Illuminist, Edmond Charles Genet, who was French envoy to the U.S. at the time. Genet was recalled to France, and he wrote to Jefferson, "Whatever, Sir, may be the result of the exploit of which you have rendered yourself the generous instrument, after having made me believe you were my friend. After having initiated me in the mysteries which have influenced my hatred against all who aspire to absolute power." One can only wonder what "mysteries" Genet had been "initiated" into by Jefferson.

The rebellion was in 1794, and in 1798 in Charlestown, South Carolina, on May 9, Rev. Jedediah Morse preached the following:

> Practically all of the civil and ecclesiastical establishments of Europe have already been shaken to their foundations by this terrible organization [the Illuminati]; the French Revolution itself is doubtless to be traced to its machinations. . . . The Jacobins are nothing more nor less than the open manifestation of the hidden system of the Illuminati. The Order has its branches established and its emissaries at work in America. The affiliated Jacobin societies in America have doubtless had as the object of their establishment the propagation of the principles of the illuminated mother club in France.

One of the primary societies established in the United States during this era was the Theistical Society, later called the Society of the Columbian Illuminati. This deistical society was founded near the beginning of the nineteenth century by Elihu Palmer in New York, and it had sister organizations in Philadelphia and Baltimore.

Column honoring Czar Alexander I has an eye above a triangle.

The Illuminati was very interested in placing their members as tutors of the children of nobility, especially princes who would later become rulers of countries. Such is the case of Alexander I of Russia, who came under the influence of the Illuminati at a young age. In St. Petersburg in the Winter Palace Square is a marble column built in 1830–1834 in honor of Czar Alexander I, and on its black granite base is "the Illuminist eye above a triangle." This is according to author William McIlhaney, who visited the Soviet Union for eight weeks in 1969 and saw the Alexander column.

The Illuminati also formed student societies at universities, for example in Germany at Tugenbund and Berschenschaften. William H. Russell matriculated through those institutions, and brought back the student societies' ceremonies and rites to Yale University, establishing the secretive Skull & Bones society there in the 1830s. The next decade, Wilhelm Weitling, a follower of the revolutionary Buonarotti and a second generation disciple of Illuminati founder Adam Weishaupt, was a leader of the League of the

Just and hired Karl Marx to write the Communist Manifesto.

Revolutionists were active in Europe during the nineteenth century, especially in Italy, where Helena Petrovna Blavatsky was wounded in the Battle of Montana near Rome on November 3, 1867. She was a member of the revolutionary Carbonari, which was led by Giuseppi Mazzini, who was known as an "established point of light when rays traversed the world." In the 1870s, she formed the Theosophical Society with an affiliate called the Order of the Round Table and a division called the Order of the Swastika. She was succeeded as head of this Society by Fabian Socialist Annie Besant (who wore a swastika), a close friend of William Stead, who was an associate of Cecil Rhodes. Rhodes was influenced by John Ruskin (who has a swastika on his gravestone), who was "reputedly a student of the Illuminati," according to award-winning author Alan Axelrod in his book *The International Encyclopedia of Secret Societies and Fraternal Orders*.

In 1891, Rhodes formed the secret "Society of the Elect" to "take the government of the whole world." Noted author Rudyard Kipling was a member of the Rhodes Trust, and he had swastikas on many of his early books.

Part of Rhodes' secret society was the semi-secret Association of Helpers, which formed Round Table groups. These groups were directed by Lord Robert Brand, who was also the managing director of Lazard Brothers. Lazard Brothers like J. P. Morgan & Company were international investment bankers who exercised control over nations' central banks, including the Federal Reserve in the U.S. Perhaps this is why President Franklin Roosevelt in 1933 wrote to Col. Edward M. House (who proposed "socialism as dreamed of by Karl Marx" in *Philip Dru: Administrator*) that "a financial element in the larger centers has owned the Government ever since the days of Andrew Jackson." Roosevelt wrote that letter after talking with international investment banker J. P. Morgan, Jr., who was the force behind the Council on Foreign Relations (CFR), which was a product of the Round Table groups. Morgan senior partner Henry P. Davison (Skull & Bones member) made Benjamin Strong vice-president of Morgan's Bankers Trust of New York, and Strong later became the first governor of the Federal Reserve Bank of New York as the joint nominee of Morgan and of Kuhn, Loeb & Company international investment bankers. Morgan was loyal to Britain, as the Bank of England in the 1800s saved his ancestor's family business. When Bank of England president Montagu Norman in the late 1920s asked Benjamin Strong to have the Federal Reserve enact policies to enable the monetary reorganization of Europe and to save the economy of England from depression, Strong was happy to oblige. These policies created inflation in the U.S. and stock market speculation which helped bring about the market's crash in October 1929. The crash marked the beginning of the Great Depression, which caused the public to accept many of President Roosevelt's socialistic programs that the power elite desired as part of Cecil Rhodes' plan.

Another part of Rhodes' society was the secret Circle of Initiates, and in Librarian of Congress James Billington's *Fire in the Minds of Men,* this Rhodes scholar wrote:

Weishaupt described his recruitment of Illuminists from within Masonic lodges in Munich as "the progress of the ☉" in the political area. He introduced italicized variants of the Latin word (*circul, circl*) into his German writings to explain the politicization of the movement, which he propagated by means of "circulars' and "circulation."

The point within a circle was also used in the first half of the twentieth century by occultist Alice Bailey, who referred to it as a "point of light," symbolizing the "solar Angel" (Lucifer). Bailey also referred to the coming "new world order."

Early in the twentieth century, World War I was precipitated in 1914 by the assassination of Austrian archduke Franz Ferdinand. The murder of the archduke was by Gavrilo Princip, an agent of the Serbian secret society called Unification or Death (also known as Narodna Odbrana, or Black Hand). This is according to Henri Pozzi's *Black Hand Over Europe,* and William McIlhaney has indicated that documents and organizational structure of this group confirm its lineage back to the Illuminati.

While the Communist views of Marx were not openly supported by many Americans in the early twentieth century, its close cousin, Socialism, and social engineering were making great headway. In the December 1933 edition of *Progressive Education,* Dr. George Hartmann of Pennsylvania State University wrote "A New Definition of the Educated Man," in which he stated:

> Some may at once protest, "What? Is education to have as one
> of its symptoms the acceptance of radical views?" The answer is
> "Yes," if radicalism means any serious endeavor to alter our so-
> cial arrangements for the better. . . . How any one with the least
> pretensions to higher education can fail to be thrilled by the
> ultimate prospects of a single world government, . . . and the
> enlightened practice of eugenics and euthenics. . . .

Hartmann was active in the Socialist Party.

Another major supporter of eugenics was Winston Churchill, who was a vice-president of the First International Congress of Eugenics in 1912. Prior to the Second World War, Churchill was First Lord of the Admiralty, and an American code and cipher clerk, Tyler Kent, in late 1939 began reading secret correspondence between Churchill and President Franklin D. Roosevelt. According to John Toland in his book *Infamy,* Kent discovered that Churchill and Roosevelt were "conniving to oust Chamberlain as Prime Minister," because both Churchill and Roosevelt were "dedicated to a genuine all-out war with Naziism." And according to author William McIlhaney, in one of the secret correspondence, Churchill told Roosevelt, "I'm half American. I am the natural person to work with you. Together we can control the world."

Relevant to the power elite's "connivance" to involve us in wars, in a speech delivered in 1933, Major-General Smedley Butler (USMC) stated:

> War is just a racket. . . . Only a small inside group knows what it is about. . . . It is conducted for the benefit of the very few at the expense of the masses. . . . I wouldn't go to war again, as I have done, to protect some lousy investment of the bankers. . . . I helped make Mexico, especially Tampico, safe for American oil interests in 1914. I helped make Haiti and Cuba a decent place for the National City Bank boys to collect revenues in. I helped in the raping of half a dozen Central American republics for the benefits of Wall Street. . . . I helped purify Nicaragua for the international banking house of Brown Brothers in 1909–1912.

. . . In China I helped see to it that Standard Oil went its way unmolested.

National City Bank and Standard Oil were controlled by the Rockefellers, and they certainly did not want people looking too closely into our entrance into and involvement in the Second World War as there had been following World War I. In that regard, historian Charles Austin Beard in "Who's to Write the History of the War?" (*Saturday Evening Post,* October 4, 1947) explained:

> The Rockefeller Foundation and the Council on Foreign Relations . . . intend to prevent, if they can, a repetition of what they call in the vernacular "the debunking journalistic campaign following World War I." Translated into precise English, this means that the Foundation and the Council do not want journalists or any other persons to examine too closely and criticize too freely the official propaganda and official statements relative to "our basic aims and activities" during World War II.

Similarly, historian Harry Elmer Barnes in his *Perpetual War for Perpetual Peace* (1953) revealed:

> It may be said, with great restraint, that, never since the Middle Ages, have there been so many powerful forces organized and alerted against the assertion and acceptance of historical truth as are active today to prevent the facts about the responsibility for the second World War. . . . Even the great Rockefeller Foundation frankly admits the subsidizing of historians to anticipate and frustrate the development of any neo-Revisionism in our time.

Of course, after wars, the power elite attempts to condition a war-weary public to accept world government. And after World War II, Spencer Tracy in the movie *State of the Union* in 1948 (the year after the United World Federalists was formed) says that in a speech to leaders of industry, he will talk about the need to redistribute our wealth internationally in some areas, and then he remarks:

> I'm gonna tell them [industry leaders] that there's only one government which is capable of handling the atomic control, world disarmament, world employment, world peace, and that's a world government. . . . The people of thirteen states started the United States of America. Well, I think that the people of that many nations are now ready to start a United States of the World . . . with one international law, one international currency, one international citizenship, and I'm gonna tell them that the Brotherhood of Man is not just an idealistic dream, but a practical necessity if man is going to survive.

It may not be a coincidence that in this same year of 1948, the University of Chicago Press published *Preliminary Draft of a World Constitution* by Robert Hutchins, Mortimer Adler, Rexford Tugwell, and others.

From 1951 to 1954, Hutchins was associate director of the Ford Foundation, whose president, H. Rowan Gaither, in 1953 said they were operating under directives from the White House "the substance of which was to the effect that we should make every effort to so alter life in the United States as to make possible a comfortable merger with the Soviet Union."

For this "comfortable merger" to occur, however, there would have to be a "New World Order." And in President George Bush's address to the U.N. General Assembly on October 1, 1990, he stated: "It is in our hands . . . to press forward to cap a historic movement towards a new world order." Note particularly the word "cap" here, especially in reference to the same President Bush's Fourth of July message in *Parade* magazine, July 2, 1989, where he said: "Look on the back of any dollar bill, and you'll see it: The Great Seal of the United States bears the motto 'novus ordo seclorum,' meaning 'a new order of the ages.'" Does this mean they are capping the pyramid on the back of the dollar bill, masonically signifying that the New World Order is here? This is simply one of many things you will not have heard from the "Babel-on-agains" from their corporate media "towers" in New York and elsewhere.

As one sign that the New World Order was in fact here, or was at least being built, the Soviet Union supposedly collapsed in the early 1990s. That is why you can see today a seven-ton statue of Lenin in Seattle, and why we have U.S. National Guard partnerships with members of the former Soviet Union (e.g., California National Guard is in partnership with the Ukraine). How's that for a "comfortable merger"?

Seven-ton bronze statue of Lenin in Seattle, Washington

And another sign was that on May 14, 2002, NATO approved a new partnership with Russia, and Russian foreign minister Igor

Ivanov, after an hour-long meeting with U.S. Secretary of State Colin Powell, pronounced: "We must now together build the new world order. . . ."

Of course, for the New World Order to work efficiently, there has to be a certain amount of control by the power elite. Relevant to this, noted author Craig Roberts on Radio Liberty (November 29, 2001) said that a senior editor at Simon & Schuster "explained [to him] about 'Operation Mockingbird' and how the CIA controlled the major publishing houses and news networks, and there was certain information that they would edit out and it would never see the light of day." Even more secretive than the CIA is the National Security Agency (NSA), and on the NSA's website is the following statement about the NSA's insignia: "The key in the eagle's talons, representing the key to security, evolves from the emblem of St. Peter the Apostle, and his power to loose and to bind. The shape of the insignia, a circle, represents perpetuity of its continuance, the symbol of eternity." Think about the NSA's "power to bind" for "eternity."

Psychologically preparing the public for greater control, it seems, is a primary function of the media. Most people reject the idea that they can be manipulated like Pavlovian dogs, but psychological techniques have been developed that are quite subtle. For example, in an article for the *Florida Forum,* I described the flashing lights and images one sees in TV ads as a psychological tool and how it works. In case there are those who doubt the technique, simply consider that in Sheila Ostrander's and Lynn Schroeder's *Superlearning,* they refer to research by American neurologist Dr. Andre Puharich with pulsed lights changing brain rhythms. And they also state that "yogis long ago developed special candles that give a fast flicker effect to change states of consciousness."

Concerning the media and means of monitoring and control over the attack of September 11, 2001, Andy Rooney on CBS's program "60 Minutes" (February 10, 2002) was talking about the need for security after the terrorist attacks of September 11, 2001, and he stated: "There's got to be something better than one of these photo IDs, a tattoo somewhere maybe. . . . I wouldn't mind having something planted permanently in my arm that would identify me."

To get to a world government, the power elite first had to establish a world/global economy, and that was facilitated by regional economic arrangements such as NAFTA (North American Free Trade Agreement), which was promoted as something that would create new jobs in the U.S. However, in 2001, the U.S. actually *lost* 1,320,000 manufacturing jobs. In a speech to business leaders in Dallas on April 16, 1999, Federal Reserve Board chairman Alan Greenspan had commented: "I regret that trade policy has been inextricably linked with job creation. We try to promote free trade on the mistaken ground that it will create jobs. . . . [But] it is difficult to find credible evidence that trade has impacted the level of total employment in this country over the long run."

Since it is clear that the U.S. is, in fact, losing a large number of manufacturing jobs as a result of NAFTA, GATT (General Agreement on Tariffs and Trade), etc., "free trade" promoters argue that new high-tech jobs are making up for other lost jobs. But look at how this works. High-tech companies often locate near cities where infrastructure already exists, but lost mill jobs in small towns mean that the town's grocers, barbers, tailors, etc., dependent upon those mill workers also may have their jobs destroyed as well. Therefore, the number of jobs lost is *greater* than just the number of factory workers laid off when a plant moves to another country.

An additional tactic of NAFTA promoters is to point to the amount of exports going from the United States to Mexico, but what they don't emphasize is that a large number of those "exports" are not going as finished products used by the average Mexican. Rather, they are materials that go to numerous factories recently built just the other side of the U.S.-Mexico border, where cheap labor produces goods sent back across the border into the U.S. It's almost as if the power elite is using Mexico as a fifty-first state, but where American labor, health, etc., regulations don't apply. Relevant to this, William R. Hawkins (Senior Fellow for National Security Studies at the U.S. Business and Industry Council) wrote in "Globalization grounded" (*Washington Times,* September 28, 2001): "Globalization is nothing more than a concept created by corporate managers who want to run transnational production and distribution networks without any government controls or accountability."

Once people from the central and southern part of Mexico have moved north into these factories, they can then easily slip across the border illegally into the U.S. Elena Poniatowska, who has taught at Harvard, Yale, Princeton, etc., has stated that "Mexico is recovering the territories yielded to the United States by means of migratory tactics." One of the organizations defending illegal Mexican migrants in the U.S. has been the Ford Foundation, and interestingly, one of its hirelings, Robert Bach, was in charge of Immigration and Naturalization policy under President Clinton.

The presence of illegal migrant workers in the U.S. is an example of how the power elite controls both ends of the political spectrum. You would think that liberals and conservatives would oppose each other on this issue, but elite conservatives support the cheap labor that illegal immigrants provide, and elite liberals support the welfare-state voting bloc these same immigrants encourage. This is why the problem of illegal immigration is never solved, because both the liberals and the conservatives in the power elite support it.

In nationally syndicated columnist Georgie Anne Geyer's March 17, 2002, article "Darkness by design for amnesty move" in the *Washington Times,* she indicated that "last week—at the precise directions of Mr. Bush—the House sneaked through a bill" granting a form of amnesty to illegal aliens. Geyer explained that part of the reason for the legislation

> is big business pushing the president to provide them with more and more cheap and compliant labor. And part of it is the White House's incredibly cynical attempt to manipulate American politics at the expense of American citizens. . . . Such mini-amnesties say to the world: "We haven't learned anything from 9/11. We still don't care a whit about who obeys ours laws—in fact, we don't obey them ourselves, not if we need dawn-to-dark laborers in California and Oregon or chicken farm laborers in Arkansas."

With the overwhelming support of Democrats, the bill passed the U.S. House 275 to 137.

On NBC's "Meet the Press" (January 13, 2002), Ralph Nader indicated that a Gore presidency would not have been different from the Bush presidency in terms of NAFTA, GATT, and American jobs going beyond our borders. Nader then remarked:

> There's a permanent corporate government operating here. The American people, whether they're liberals or conservatives, feel that they've lost control over everything that matters to them— their government, their elections, . . . their genes, their privacy, their workplace, their children, commercialization of childhood. And they have a thirst for taking control again.

Nader next referred to "the concentration of power that is keeping our country down, keeping America down in terms of a prosperous, just society to hand over to future generations." Isn't the term "corporate government" another name for fascism, but this time on a global scale? The idea is that eventually the regional trading arrangements such as NAFTA (Canada, Mexico, and the U.S.), Mercosur (Argentina, Brazil, Paraguay, and Uruguay), the EU (nations of Europe), ASEAN (which includes seven countries of Southeast Asia), etc., will be merged into a final world/global economic arrangement. In the (New Age) *World Goodwill Newsletter* (No. 1, 1998) under :"Re-Thinking Globalization," one reads: "Provided that the possibility of conflict between the separate trading areas can be avoided, then hopefully they can eventually merge, and can harmonize their arrangements so that goods and services can flow freely throughout the world." World Goodwill is a service activity of Lucis Trust (a U.N. NGO with offices in London, Geneva, and at 120 Wall Street in New York City), formerly Lucifer Publishing. Once the trading areas merge, then the power elite will claim that the new world/global economic arrangement has to be enforced/managed by a world Socialist government.

In terms of GATT, one should remember that in Richard Gardner's *Foreign Affairs* article of April 1974, where he talked about eroding national sovereignty piece-by-piece, this Rhodes scholar also described how GATT could be part of the process. In addition to GATT, author and certified financial planner Joan Veon has explained how in 1980, the Monetary Control Act allowed Americans to invest overseas, and other major nations acted similarly, so that national financial borders were torn down. The result of this is that today, $1.8 trillion moves around the world *daily*. Furthermore, in 1999, the Glass-Steagall Act was repealed, allowing foreign banks to buy American banks. Moreover, the *New York Times* on the front page, February 18, 2002, published "U.S. Corporations Are Using Bermuda to Slash Tax Bills: Profits Over Patriotism." This article indicated that a growing number of American companies are incorporating in Bermuda to lower their taxes sharply without giving up benefits of doing business in the U.S. (the working headquarters of the companies are kept in the U.S.). This saves the companies hundreds of millions of dollars in income taxes, but that means a greater proportion of taxes is paid by other taxpayers.

These are all consequences of economic globalization, which is usually portrayed as being opposed by "right-wing America First" types. However, there are prominent liberals who oppose many of its aspects as well. For example, on June 6, 2000, former Canadian deputy prime minister Paul Hellyer (author of *The Evil Empire: Globalization's Darker Side*) addressed the Ontario Club with the following words:

. . . We are losing control over our lives and destiny. . . . The bad globalization is unrestricted capital flows and the unrelenting concentration of ownership and industrial and financial power in fewer and fewer hands. This kind of globalization is agenda driven. It is an attempt by a relatively small number of international banks and transnational corporations centered largely in the five major industrial powers to take over governance of the world for their own benefit. . . . It may be advertised as the road to Nirvana but, in my opinion, it is the highway to poverty, homelessness, and disease for tens of millions of the earth's inhabitants. . . . In reality it is the ascendancy of monopoly economics on a world scale. We are losing control of our most important industries. . . . Globalization is really a code word for corporate rule and colonization. . . . Lewis Lapham, editor of *Harper's Magazine,* says the U.S. has two governments—the permanent government and the provisional government. The permanent government comprises: (a) the Fortune 500 list of the largest American corporations; (b) the largest law firms in Washington that do their legal work for them; (c) the largest public relations firms in Washington that do their advertising and public relations; and (d) the top public servants, both civil and military. These groups make up the permanent government which really runs the country. Then there is the provisional government—"politicians for hire." Every few years there is a charade called an election, which picks a political actor to go on stage and read the scripts written by the permanent government. As some actors read scripts with less improvisation than others, the permanent government checks them out in advance and decides who they want. Then they put up the money to get them elected. . . . In a globalized society, people don't matter—

only corporations do. Small independent operators and family farms are doomed by globalization. . . . Globalization in agriculture means three or four giant agribusinesses are determined to monopolize the world food supply with their genetically altered species and make us all dependent on them for our food. . . . Canada and the world are being re-engineered without the consent of the citizens who are having their birthrights sold out from under their feet.

Hellyer's views are supported in Richard Longworth's article, "Government without Democracy: The global economy is well governed—in the interest of the elite," in *The American Prospect* (Summer 2001). Longworth is a senior writer for the *Chicago Tribune,* and in this article, he explained:

Government officials and international experts—often helped by the very industries and corporations they seek to regulate— are weaving a legal and supervisory web around the global economy. Nonbinding standards to promote uniformity in banking, accounting, and corporate behavior become templates of good conduct and take on the force of law. Most insidiously, this governance grows by the day, even without new rules and laws. Often, old national rules and laws are interpreted or bent by regulators, to the point that differences between national codes are shaded or even erased. In the process, a new global law comes into being, to be enforced by the same people who created it. These new global rule-makers are well on their way to legislating the twenty-first century. . . . The crisis, then, is not global anarchy, nor a lack of laws, nor the weakness of national governments. It is the growing code of global laws—often written by representatives of national governments and enforced by regulators from those governments—that supersede national laws and increasingly govern the lives of citizens who have no say in how they are written.

A recent example of how this mechanism operates can be seen in the *Wall Street Journal* editorial "Pandora's Trade War" (January 17, 2002), which described "a tale of how the World Trade Organization has run amok." The editorial continued: "This spat has become testy this week with the WTO's $4 billion ruling in favor of Europe's objection to a U.S. law that gives a tax break to exporters who operate through offshore subsidiaries." The editorial ends by criticizing the WTO for trying "to be a world supergovernment that trumps national tax policies."

The concept of a "world supergovernment" is not only effecting the U.S., but the nations of Europe as well, with the interim state being the creation of a European superstate undermining national sovereignty. In George Will's "A Superstate of Blandness" (*Washington Post,* December 30, 2001), he explained the consequences of the introduction of the "euro" (adopted by European nations except Britain, Denmark, and Sweden) as follows:

> The common currency serves the political objective of changing Europe's civic discourse by supplanting political reasoning with economic calculation. The euro is an instrument for producing a European superstate, which requires erasing from the nations' populations their national identities. . . . Under the euro, nations cede fundamental attributes of sovereignty—control of

monetary (and hence, effectively, fiscal) policy to the European Central Bank in Frankfurt. This advances the integration of Europe's nations into a continental federation, under which nations will be as "sovereign" as Louisiana and Idaho are. . . . Who wants the euro and the superstate it implies? The EU's disparate publics do not, but two elites do. One is a commercial elite that believes the business of Europe is business—never mind freedom, democracy, justice, culture, different national characters—and that a common currency will expedite it a bit. The other elite consists of the sort of intellectuals Europe has always had a surplus of—those eager to remake mankind in order to make it worthy of the shimmering future the intellectuals are dreaming up. . . . The euro is part of the EU's campaign for the dissolution of nations.

Supporting what George Will said about the European Central Bank are the remarks of Center for Strategic and International Studies Senior Fellow Edward Luttwak in his 1999 book, *Turbo Capitalism: Winners and Losers in the Global Economy*. In that book, he explained:

No independence can be as magnificently absolute as that of the European Central Bank itself: it is to receive no instructions from either member countries or any institution of the European Union. . . . This is truly a sovereign power, given irrevocably to an institution headed by a central banker, selected and advised by other central bankers, who are themselves recruited and trained by their predecessors in their respective central banks. This non-elected European Central Bank will assume total and exclusive control over the monetary policy of all

member countries. . . . Itself free of any democratic interfer-
ence, the Bank will be free to interfere at will in all that con-
cerns money in all the member countries.

And applauding the structure of the European Union, Robert
Muller, former assistant secretary-general of the U.N., wrote in
2000 Ideas for a Better World:

Being a remarkable model of a new world order, much better
than the U.N., the European Union should help the world create a Commission or group of eminent thinkers to offer a plan
for the transformation of the United Nations into a true World
Union.

That Britain did not formally adopt the euro at this time does not
mean British sovereignty is not threatened. Prime Minister Tony
Blair's foreign secretary, Jack Straw, in a November 22, 2001, article in *The Independent* (England) wrote that

in a world where states and the interests of their citizens are so
obviously interdependent, we need to rethink our attitudes to
concepts like "independence" and "sovereignty." . . . Sovereignty
has always been a relative concept—since it defines the position
of a nation in relation to other nations and peoples. . . . We pool
sovereignty in the United Nations, where Security Council reso-
lutions have the force of international law. . . . Tomorrow [No-
vember 23], in a speech in Birmingham [to the European Research Institute], the Prime Minister will be making the case
once again for strengthening our sovereignty by pooling it, where
we choose to. . . .

Further evidence that Blair would "pool sovereignty in the United Nations" can be found at the beginning of *The Independent* (Britain) article, "Blair says no attack on Iraq without UN consent" (May 10, 2002), by Andrew Grice and Davis Usborne, which states: "Tony Blair has privately reassured his Labour Party critics that Britain will not back U.S. military actions against Iraq unless it wins the backing of the United Nations Security Council." Ultimately, the oxymoron of "pooling" nations' "sovereignty" in the United Nations will be a major step toward a world government.

Writing about the problems of globalization on his website (*http://perso.infonie.be/le.feu*) late in 2001, Michel Schooyans (professor emeritus at Louvain University in Belgium) explained that

> positive international law is the instrument used by the U.N. to organize the global world society. Under cover of globalization, the U.N. organizes world "governance" for its own benefit. Under cover of "shared responsibility," it has invited the states (nations) to limit their proper sovereignty. The U.N. globalizes by increasingly posing as a worldwide superstate. It is tending to regulate all the dimensions of life, of thought and human activity by establishing a progressively centralized control of information, of knowledge and techniques, of foodstuffs, of human life, of health and of population, of surfaces and subsoil resources, of world commerce and union organizations, finally and above all, of politics and law. Its power is not only increasingly expanded; it integrates the factors—political, economic, psychosocial, and military—that constitute it, as in the doctrine of national security. Exalting the neo-pagan cult of Mother Earth, it deprives man of the central place accorded him in the great

traditions of philosophy, law, politics, and religion. . . . Before the impossible "cohesion" and "globalization" that the U.N. is striving to impose by inciting an always precarious "consensus," the Church must appear, following Christ's example, as a sign of division. . . . Before the emergence of a new Leviathan, we cannot remain mute, inactive, or indifferent.

In the American Family Association's *AFA Journal* (March 2002), Belgian official Pascal Smet was quoted as saying: "It's a basic rule of management that if you want to manage something, you measure it. It's the same with human beings and migration." The *AFA Journal* further indicated that Smet in December 2001 made a proposal at a U.N. meeting that suggests the implementation of a system which would require the fingerprinting and registration of every person in the world. Smet noted that the European Union was already considering a similar Europe-wide system, which would use either fingerprints or eye-scanning technology to identify citizens.

To show how the U.N. plans to further its goals, one might first look at the Millennium Development Goals (MDG) endorsed by one hundred eighty-nine countries at the September 2000 U.N. Millennium General Assembly. For example, to "promote gender equality and empower women," the U.N. will monitor the "share of women in wage employment in the nonagricultural sector" and the "proportion of seats held by women in national parliament." To see how well countries "integrate the principles of sustainable development into country policies and programs," the U.N. will monitor such things as the "proportion of land area covered by forest" and "land area protected to maintain biological diversity."

And to "develop a global partnership for development," the U.N.'s MDGs included as targets: "develop further an open, rule-based, predictable, nondiscriminatory trading and financial system" and "in cooperation with developing countries, develop and implement strategies for decent and productive work for youth."

On September 19, 2001, the U.N. secretary-general issued a report, "'Road Map' of Millennium Summit Goals Sets Out Blueprint, Timetable for Future Implementation." Secretary-General Kofi Annan said:

> The entire United Nations family of Member States, international organizations, funds, agencies, programs, the private sector and civil society must join together to meet the lofty commitments that are embodied in the Millennium Declaration . . . including strengthening the rule of law, and taking action against transnational crime by helping States ratify treaties and harmonize their domestic laws with international obligations. . . . Other proactive measures include widening the jurisdiction of the International Court of Justice and promoting the rapid entry into force of the Rome Statute of the International Criminal Court. . . . Of overriding importance is the need to pursue disarmament in all areas. . . . It is crucial that the MDGs become national goals. . . . [The report] advocates support for efforts to implement the Convention on the Rights of the Child. . . .

Now the U.N. has issued many reports in the past, and people have generally not worried much about them because the U.N. has lacked sufficient enforcement mechanisms. However, on the same day (September 19, 2001) the U.N. secretary-general's report mentioned above was issued, the World Bank announced that it was "joining the United Nations as a full partner in implementing the MDGs." Eduardo Doryan, the World Bank's special representative to the U.N., stated: "By joining the U.N. in implementing the MDGs, the Bank aims to put the goals at the heart of its development agenda. Having a well-crafted set of goals, targets, and indicators emphasizes the importance of monitoring performance against outcomes and adopting effective means of reaching agreed goals."

Thus, with the World Bank's ability to provide or withhold funds based upon nations' willingness to implement the MDGs, the U.N.'s efforts to increase its power via the MDGs becomes troubling indeed. At a press conference on April 19, 2002, World Bank president James Wolfensohn remarked:

> We have started a website called Global Gateway [and] have now listed 400,000 projects in the last years that are being implemented or have been implemented around the world. . . . I think there is a growing understanding that education is the number one priority. . . . Let's look at the effectiveness generally of aid in terms of it allowing us to reach the Millennium Development Goals. . . . We are definitely looking at the question of educational content, and we are starting with a very simple notion that if we can train the kids in basic skills, give them a sense of global as well as national citizenship, . . . that will be a pretty good start. . . . I think the important thing about this initiative is that it goes beyond measuring attendance in schools just with numbers and looks at both content and continuity. . . .

Relevant to the New Age concept of "Mother Earth" mentioned earlier by Professor Schooyans, according to "Cherie stops Blair being stick in the mud" (*London Times,* December 15, 2001), deputy political editor Tom Baldwin related how last August, Prime Minister Tony Blair (a vice-president of Socialist International) and his wife, Cherie, tried "a New Age experience on the Mexican Riviera, rubbing fruit and mud over each other's bodies and making a wish for 'world peace.'" Baldwin wrote that they were "invited to meditate, feel at one with Mother Earth, and experience inner feelings and visions." The Blairs bowed and prayed to the four winds as Mayan prayers were read, and before leaving the steam bath, they were told to scream out loud to signify the pain of rebirth. Baldwin further related that Cherie Blair has a bioelectric shield pendant filled with "magic crystals," and that she has been a client of Bharti Vyas, a New Age wholistic therapy guru in London.

Relevant to Prime Minister Blair and the New Age, he is perhaps best noted for his "Third Way" (combining Socialism and capitalism), and in leading New Ager Alice Bailey's *The Rays and the Initiations,* she wrote years ago that "in Great Britain, the problem of socialism is being resolved and the sound judgment of the people will eventually balance the two conditions of a socialist programme and free enterprise." Bailey's theosophical occultist predecessor was Annie Besant (co-editor of *Lucifer* magazine with Madame Helena Petrovna Blavatsky), an early leader of the Fabian Socialists. The Fabian Society has printed Blair's essays on "The Third Way."

Not only do Fabian Socialists like Tony Blair talk about "The Third Way," but so do Rhodes scholars like Bill Clinton. And in case anyone doesn't believe that people like Blair and Clinton have been groomed by the power elite, such as the Bilderbergers, tell them to read the following Reuters article, "Secretive Bilderberg group to meet in Sweden," by Peter Starck on May 23, 2001, which stated:

> The Bilderberg Group, a semi-secret discussion forum for the Western world's power elite, will hold its annual meeting . . . on May 24–28. . . . Today, many critics see it as a conspiracy and an agent of a new capitalist world order. . . . Invited speakers, Bill Clinton and Tony Blair, were groomed at Bilderberg meetings before rising to fame as U.S. President and British Prime Minister respectively.

Why is it important that both Blair and Clinton emphasize "The Third Way"? It is because the world government toward which the U.N. is leading us will be a world Socialist government, synthesizing Western capitalism and Eastern Communism. For years, the power elite has been promoting a world Socialist government. The Center for War/Peace Studies (with board sponsors such as Brock Chisolm and ACLU founder Roger Baldwin, a Communist) has published *The War/Peace Report,* and in its August/September 1969 edition is "The Bankruptcy of the Peace Movement" by W. Warren Wagar, associate professor of history at the University of New Mexico. In this article, Wagar declared:

> The idea of a federal world government kindled the imagination even of statesmen. . . . What we seek is a federal union of an order of magnitude without precedent in history. . . . Only socialism has ever seriously established itself both at the national and international level, in pursuit of revolutionary world trans-

> formation. . . . We need an ideology of world integration. . . .
> Never forget that we are seeking to abolish the sovereign na-
> tion-state system and to build a new [world] civilization. . . . To
> a very considerable degree, the world political party may have
> to operate underground. . . . It may be more interested in the
> permeation of government bureaus, universities, newspapers,
> and corporations than in playing parliamentary politics.

In addition to the globalist power elite's synthesis of capitalism
and Communism into a world Socialist government, religions will
be synthesized as well into a one-world religion based upon what
John Dewey called a "common faith." The reason religion cannot
be left out of the power elite's plan for a world Socialist government can be found in Fabian Society member Walter Rauschenbusch's 1893 statement: "The only power that can make socialism
succeed, if it is established, is religion." On December 2, 1908,
Rauschenbusch co-founded the Federal Council of Churches,
which would later be called the National Council of Churches,
part of the World Council of Churches, which is dominated by
Socialists, just as is the United Nations today.

But what if traditional Bible-believing Christians object to the
power elite's control? They will simply be labelled as "hate mongers." And if you don't think that can happen, the West Virginia
Register-Herald (September 2, 2001) printed an article, "Christians
a 'Hate Group,'" describing a teaching manual crafted by former
U.S. attorney-general Janet Reno which identifies "hate mongers"
as those who "blame the federal government [and others] for most
of this country's problems. Some groups include apocalyptic Chris-
tianity in their ideology and believe we are in, or approaching, a

period of violence and social turmoil which will precede the Second Coming of Christ."

Are we in a period of violence in the Middle East that could eventually precede the Second Coming of Christ? Zechariah was the prophet who urged rebuilding the Temple, and in Zechariah 12:2-3, 9–11, one reads:

> Behold, I will make Jerusalem a cup of trembling unto all the people round about, when they shall be in the siege both against Judah and against Jerusalem. And in that day will I make Jerusalem a burdensome stone for all people: all that burden themselves with it shall be cut in pieces, though all the people of the earth be gathered together against it. . . . And it shall come to pass in that day, that I will seek to destroy all the nations that come against Jerusalem. And I will pour upon the house of David, and upon the inhabitants of Jerusalem, the spirit of grace and of supplications: and they shall look upon me whom they have pierced, and they shall mourn for him, as one mourneth for his only son, . . . In that day shall there be a great mourning in Jerusalem, as the mourning of Hadadrimmon in the valley of Megiddon.

Note the relevance to the U.N. ("all the people of the earth") pressuring Israel today, to Jesus ("whom they have pierced"), and to Armageddon ("in the valley of Megiddon").

Then what could happen to these "hate mongers" mentioned above? Perhaps legal action could be taken, because on November 16, 1995, the members of UNESCO signed the "Declaration of

Principles on Tolerance," which stated that tolerance "is not only a moral duty, it is also a political and legal requirement." The declaration indicates that tolerance means actual "acceptance" of forms of expression, and "it involves the rejection of dogmatism and absolutism. . . . It is necessary to promote systematic and rational tolerance teaching methods that will address the . . . religious sources of intolerance." So, those Christians who have religious dogmas or believe in moral absolutes could be in legal trouble in the future if UNESCO's declaration were to be enforced. Remember that Matthew 10:17–18 says: "But beware of men: for they will deliver you up to the councils, and they will scourge you in their synagogues; And ye shall be brought before governors and kings for my sake, for a testimony against them and the Gentiles."

Some might respond to this by saying, "But Americans have constitutional protections to guard them." But do we really? A headline in the *Oakland* (Michigan) *Press* (April 24, 2002) stated: "The state Legislature has given police power to search your home without telling why." The title of the article above this headline is "Living in a police state," and the article revealed:

> Two new laws, which took effect Monday as part of anti-terror efforts, also shield from public scrutiny the reasons for police searches. . . . Defense lawyer Walter Piszczatowski said: "This is nuts, this is beyond nuts. What happened to the Fourth Amendment? We're living in a police state." That means the public, the press, and in some cases even the person accused of the crime, can't know why the police entered a home without permission. . . . The House portion of the bill passed unanimously and the Senate version passed 27–8.

Not only does the U.N. want legal action taken regarding religious and other "intolerance," but in the area of war crimes as well. In that regard, reporter Tom Carter in the March 28, 2002, *Washington Times* wrote: "The International Criminal Court is on track to become a reality by mid-April, claiming a mandate to indict and try anyone in the world, including Americans, U.N. officials and supporters said yesterday. . . . The court . . . claims jurisdiction even over citizens of countries that do not ratify the treaty." On April 11, the International Criminal Court (ICC) did, in fact, receive the necessary votes to become a reality. Now, even if the U.S. doesn't ratify the treaty, the U.N.'s ICC claims the right to indict and try Americans anyway. Anyone who says we are not fast approaching a world government, remind them of this, and tell them to read the views of Richard A. Falk concerning this matter. Falk has been a consultant to the U.S. Senate Foreign Relations Committee, a Ford Foundation Fellow, a Fellow with the (New Age) Lindisfarne Association, a Senior Fellow with the Institute for World Order, a member of the Planetary Citizens Advisory Council, and a member of the Council on Foreign Relations. In an article, "Next, a global parliament" (*International Herald Tribune,* April 19, 2002), co-authored by Falk, he stated:

> A . . . regressive vision has been gaining momentum in the aftermath of Sept. 11 and in the course of the horrifying encounter in the Middle East. This is a vision of the world order that continues to be dominated by sovereign states which put their selfish interests and subjective claims above the rules of international law or the common good. . . . In a period of heightened tensions, it leads to . . . nationalism. . . . Promoting the promise

of the International Criminal Court and avoiding this alternative future should be the overriding strategic priority of those committed to a better future for humanity. . . . But we must also move beyond the court as a stand-alone project to build the other institutions upon which law can function. A most timely initiative would be to move mountains to establish a functioning global parliament. . . . Surely, with the power of popular sovereignty behind it, the Global Parliament would, like the European Parliament, grow in power and stature over time.

Already, the U.N.'s International Criminal Tribunal for War Crimes in the former Yugoslavia has claimed the right to apprehend and forcibly take former Yugoslav leader Slobodan Milosevic to the Hague for trial. Concerning this, anti-Communist Yugoslav Aleksandar Pavic, writing for *WorldNetDaily* (April 8, 2002) from Belgrade, stated:

These U.S. officials are coming into a sovereign country—although the concept of sovereignty is fast becoming obsolete under the New Order—to demand compliance with a "court" that could never pass muster in the United States as long as it is still a free and democratic land. For the International Criminal Tribunal for War Crimes in the former Yugoslavia is an institution that is both judge and prosecutor, that is financed by foreign governments, that allows anonymous witnesses, that uses NATO troops to hunt down "suspects" even in their own countries with brutal force and that has no jury. . . . This "court" is the perfect example of how the law can be used as a bludgeon of political control and foreign policy. . . . And the U.S. is throwing its substantial diplomatic and political weight behind this institution. The question is why? Is it because it is the model of the future that needs legitimization abroad before it can be applied at home? If so, then Americans should take heed and follow its proceedings. . . . Old Yugoslav anti-Communists, this writer included, feel that they did not fight so that one brand of totalitarianism would be replaced by another—either locally or globally. For, the Hague proceedings are in fact a show trial reminiscent of the banner days of Joe Stalin. And the question that still remains is—why is the U.S. promoting this?

Good question, and Americans should think long and hard about it.

Why should we think about it? It's because the U.N. may be setting precedents for intervening in other nations as well. For example, in late April 2002, U.N. Secretary-General Kofi Annan appointed Finnish pathologist Dr. Helena Ranta as an advisor investigating whether the Israelis conducted a "massacre" in Jenin. According to Associated Press writer Steve Weizman in Jerusalem in "Jenin 'war crimes' revealed" (*The Advertiser,* Adelaide, Australia, May 4, 2002): "The U.S.-based Human Rights Watch says Israeli troops may have committed war crimes at the Jenin refugee camp last month, but there is no evidence to support Palestinian claims of a massacre." As evidence of U.N. bias against Israel, the Israelis point to the fact that the U.N. has not launched an investigation of Palestinian terrorist activities against Israelis.

Dr. Ranta is the same head of the European Union's Forensic Expert Team that investigated whether Yugoslav armed forces massacred Albanian civilians in the Kosovo village of Raca on January

15, 1999. On March 17, 1999, Dr. Ranta said "crimes against humanity" had been committed in Raca, and a week later, NATO
began seventy-eight days of bombing against Yugoslavia. Milosevic
and others on May 22, 1999, were indicted for this and other crimes,
but in Aleksander Pavic's April 29, 2002, column for *WorldNetDaily*,
he wrote that the full report of Ranta's team "was suppressed by
the U.N. and the EU for a full two years, until February 2001.
When it was finally published in *Forensic Science International,* the
report revealed that there was no evidence of a massacre."

The U.N. is particularly interested in the conflict in the Middle
East, because only when peoples such as the Israelis and Palestinian Arabs cannot resolve their problems might they turn for help
to the U.N. as a type of world government. On the one hand,
there are the Arab terrorist suicide bombers murdering innocent
Israeli civilians. On the other hand, *New York Times* reporter Chris
Hedges in *Harper's Magazine* (October 2001) described Israeli soldiers saying to Arabs through a loudspeaker: "Come on, dogs.
Where are all the dogs of Khan Younis? Come! Come! Son of a
bitch! Son of a whore!" And when Arab children responded by
throwing rocks at the soldiers, they were shot with silencers. Hedges
writes: "I have never before watched soldiers entice children like
mice into a trap and murder them for sport."

If the U.N. can intervene in the conflict between Israelis and
Palestinian Arabs, a major step will have been taken toward the
acceptance of a world government. And in case anyone thinks the
U.N. is really going to do something to stop terrorism, it should
be remembered that less than one month after the terrorist attacks
upon America on September 11, 2001, Syria was named to the
U.N. Security Council on October 8, even though Syria is on the

U.S. government's list of nations that sponsor terrorism.

Unfortunately, many people professing to be Christians are spending too much of their time pursuing fun and pleasure, waiting to be raptured because they say they have "accepted" Jesus as their Lord and Savior. However, Christ said in Matthew 10:38: "And he that taketh not his cross, and followeth after me, is not worthy of me."

Be careful not to be deceived. Be informed, and inform others. Pray for our leaders, and when needed, and in an appropriate manner, remind the president and members of Congress of the words of their solemn "Oath of Office." Their oath requires them to "defend the *Constitution of the United States,*" and this means not undermining our national sovereignty by deferring to the U.N. or the World Trade Organization, or by moving us toward world government.

Pray for America and for souls everywhere.

About the Author

Dennis Laurence Cuddy, historian and political analyst, received a Ph.D. from the University of North Carolina at Chapel Hill (major in American History, minor in Political Science), and taught in the public school system and at the university level. Dr. Cuddy has authored or edited fifteen books and booklets, authored hundreds of articles appearing in newspapers around the nation, and served as a senior associate with the U.S. Department of Education in Washington. He has been a guest on numerous radio talk shows in various parts of the country, such as ABC-Radio in New York City, and he has also been a guest on the national television programs "USA Today" and CBS' "Nightwatch."

"Compellingly important knowledge gained from reading this
meticulously documented book is vital for everyone's discern-
ment in these critical times."

—Dr. Shirley M. Correll, Pro-Family Forum, Florida

Now Is the Dawning of the New Age New World Order is a chronology
covering events and characters having dramatic consequences in
history. In their own words, the gradual unfolding of the New Age
New World Order is presented.

". . . the most comprehensive coverage of the New World Order/
New Age movement available today."

—Robert H. Golsborough, editor, *Washington Dateline*

ISBN 1-57558-059-4 $12.95

Hearthstone Publishing, Ltd.
toll-free: 1-888-891-3300   e-mail: *hearthstone@coxinet.net*

In 1890 Cecil Rhodes stated that he would start a movement that would in 100 years bring in a world government in which there would be no war and only one language. One hundred years later in 1990, President Bush announced the arrival of the New World Order.

Since early this century Rhodes scholars have been involved with the CFR, United Nations, International Monetary Fund, international banking, Congress, and federal administrations since Woodrow Wilson. President Bill Clinton, a Rhodes scholar, appointed at least twenty-two Rhodes scholars to high positions in his administration. Dr. Dennis Cuddy reveals the source of the conspiracy that has been dedicated to erasing nationalism and replacing it with a world government.

ISBN 1-57558-031-4 $11.95

Hearthstone Publishing, Ltd.
toll-free: 1-888-891-3300   **e-mail: *hearthstone@coxinet.net***

Many people today laugh at conspiracy theories, saying "Where's the positive proof?" This book (as well as its predecessor, *Secret Records Revealed*) attempts not only to lay before the reader positive testimony but also to provide a vast amount of circumstantial evidence that cannot lie in demonstrating that a power elite has been attempting to gain more and more control over events in the world.

If *Secret Records Revealed* could be called "Untaught History 101," then *The Globalists* should be considered "Untaught History 102."

ISBN 1-57558-086-1 $14.95

Hearthstone Publishing, Ltd.
toll-free: 1-888-891-3300   **e-mail:** *hearthstone@coxinet.net*

The National Education Association is the driving force that channels—through public education—humanistic political beliefs into the minds of the vast majority of our children.

Every parent, every patriotic American citizen, needs to be fully informed how present and future generations are indoctrinated in "progressive" education by the NEA, which has promoted world government.

This book is a bombshell.

ISBN 1-57558-052-7 $7.95

Hearthstone Publishing, Ltd.
toll-free: 1-888-891-3300   **e-mail:** *hearthstone@coxinet.net*